DEAR JESUS, SEND COFFEE

Finding Joy in the Chaos of Early Motherhood

DEAR JESUS, SEND COFFEE

FINDING JOY IN THE CHAOS
OF EARLY MOTHERHOOD

MEREDITH REDMON

NEW DEGREE PRESS

COPYRIGHT © 2021 MEREDITH REDMON

Cover Photography by Haley Kinzie

DEAR JESUS, SEND COFFEE
Finding Joy in the Chaos of Early Motherhood

ISBN   978-1-63730-323-8 *Paperback*
            978-1-63730-324-5 *Kindle Ebook*
            978-1-63730-325-2 *Ebook*

To the mothers that shaped me.

Table of Contents

INTRODUCTION

———

"When God is going to do something wonderful, He or She always starts with a hardship; when God is going to do something amazing, He or She starts with an impossibility."

—ANNE LAMOTT, PLAN B: FURTHER THOUGHTS ON FAITH

It only takes a quick Google search to see that the internet is saturated with motherhood how-tos: "How to make my baby sleep," "How to want to have sex again after a baby," or, most annoyingly, "How to be the perfect mother." Women adding their two cents to the ups and downs of parenting.

Why is this? From a combination of my own experience and conducting interviews, new moms are looking for two things: connection and regaining their sense of self after the birth of children. They ask, "Who was I before I wore the same stained yoga pants three days in a row?" and, maybe more importantly, "Can someone tell me who invented dry shampoo, so I can send them a Christmas card?"

In speaking to parents while researching this book, I learned that if you start labor having memorized *What to Expect*

When You're Expecting verbatim or you wing the whole enchilada, the result will be the same—a shock unlike any other. For example, on the first night home from the hospital with my newborn son, I looked around the room at 2 a.m., helpless. I saw my comatose husband, whom I could not blame for snoozing, yet I still resented his useless nipples. As a pediatric ICU nurse of many years and an ER doctor, we were surely qualified to raise a child. But in that moment, all I could think to myself was, *Can I get a real grown-up in here? And who the heck said breastfeeding was natural? This ish hurts! Can I please get an adultier-adult up in here?*

The incidence of maternal mental health disorders is on the rise. At least one in eight women experiences postpartum depression, and matching statistics reveal similar frequency with postpartum anxiety, according to the National Institutes of Health (NIH). Really, who could blame us? Not only are we entering motherhood with way, way too much conflicting information, but we are also starting families, on average later. Often, fertility challenges, work-life balance, and extended family expectations lead to a stressful environment right from the minute we decide to become parents. Currently, fertility challenges and age restraints may play a bigger role in how many children we decide to have than it has in past decades.

Many women also have to fight the "having it all" conundrum in a world that makes such a dream impossible. There are only twenty-four hours in a day. For women with more education or careers, choosing how to balance finances and allocate childcare responsibilities with a partner can be a challenge. Those of us growing up in the *Boy Meets World* era saw sitcom moms who either made chocolate chip cookies on the daily or worked high-powered careers, but they were still always there to have the perfect mother-child chat set to a '90s ballad. We begin parenting with the expectation that if we want to be excellent parents, we will make it happen. What precious little idiots we were—thinking the desire to be a good mother would somehow make motherhood easy.

I felt like I needed a calling to pull me out of the daily grind of diapers and a second pregnancy, so I threw my hat in the ring for a contributor position at the *Oklahoma City Mom* blog. Many of the other mothers whom I worked with had personal blogs with great reach. I loved the idea of being able to retain the rights to my own words, so Motherhood by Meredith was born.

As I began blogging, I wondered whether this approach to reclaiming a sense of pre-baby self was unique or if it was a process we could all learn to do. Can we redefine ourselves in the midst of the chaos of early motherhood? Was finding a passion my ticket to finding myself again?

Upon researching and interviewing women on paths which were similar to my own, I came to realize that many of us share core insecurities: how we get pregnant and birth our babies, how our families sleep, how we feed our children, the style of parenting we choose, and how our children reach milestones compared to others. There are personal, societal, and cultural reasons why these insecurities and mismatches between expectation and reality occur.

The good news is that there is hope. We are not stuck in a loop. We can cultivate a beautiful life within the blueprint of God's plan for us feeling joyful and fulfilled.

None of us want to admit that we, in fact, "don't got this." Self judgement paralyzes us. Maybe this is where the dreaded mommy wars stem from; we are too caught up in trying to figure out our own messes that we draw lines out of insecurity instead of building communities. (More on that later.)

The beauty of parenting, however, is that our kids are raising us as we raise them, and the perfectly filtered world of Instagram #motherhood is not reality. We learn from our mistakes, but by getting up each morning and trying to be better, we are excellent parents. The perfect mother doesn't really exist.

Throughout this book, I'll share my own journey in embarrassing but relatable detail: how I slowly built confidence through tears, lots of prayers, and many, many mistakes. Enough to do it all over again The second time wasn't exactly *easier,* as they still expect you to care for your first child when you birth another—go figure. But I will say I figured it out in a winding, messy, beautiful path that I now know is early motherhood. I have bounced back, not into my pre-pregnancy pants, but into my figuring out my new self-identity.

If you are a new mama or thinking about littles, grab a latte or glass of pinot. This book is for you. I'll dive into how our expectations and reality don't really mesh as well as how the most beautiful motherhood moments are often the messiest. I'll also share how to put your hair in a semi-clean top knot and find the woman you're designed to be through interviews with experts and real mamas.

In this book, we will explore how to find your new definition of a post-baby self, learn about Alexandra Sacks' groundbreaking research on the concept of *matrescence*, which compares the hormonal and role changes of early motherhood to those of adolescence. We will focus on how to create a support network and actually reach out those we trust instead of drowning in your own perfectionism. Finally, we'll focus on how to cultivate a spiritual relationship with a higher power—whatever that may look like for you. The idea behind this book is to provide refreshing takes on the current state of motherhood, how to transcend expectations, and reclaiming your identity.

HOW TO USE THIS BOOK

———

Hey y'all,

First, I want to state that I am writing this book from my own motherhood experience. If it is very different from yours, that's okay by me. Just as there are billions of mothers on the planet, there are billions of ways to mother. My hope is that our differences fail to compete with the common ground we share. I would never pretend to be able to speak to parenting experiences I have not had. To do that would be to overshadow the voices women who are living different truths. Even if we have nothing in common on paper, we all share many facets of parenting.

This book is divided into three sections: insecurities we all face, why we face them, and what to do about them. Here's the deal. Not one of us knows what we are doing. Yep, even that mom in playgroup who shows up with perfect hair and clean kids in monogramed outfits to every play date. She's as clueless and insecure as you are. But like you, she is the right mom for her own kids. Like you, she has likely fallen prey to the same set of insecurities. We all face them. From talking to hundreds of women and reading about even more, I have discovered certain truths about early motherhood. Most of us are concerned about the following:

- How we got pregnant and gave birth, which is why women love to tell every last detail of their birth stories.

- How we feed our babies, which is why breastfeeding badges are a thing and hashtags like #fedisbest go viral.

- How our kids sleep. Are you pro- or anti-Dr. Ferber?

- What style of parenting we choose. You know each decision you make basically influences your child's likelihood of belonging to a prison gang.

But here's the deal, Mama. It's not your fault. It's both nature and nurture. We'll explore contributing factors like engrained social norms, personality type, hormones, and a fun new term called "matrescence." Additionally, you don't have to feel stuck on this hamster wheel of sleep deprivation and feelings of inadequacy. I have been there too, so I know you can find your joy not by squeezing your body into a pair of jeans from high school or drinking a shake sold to you by someone you knew when you wore said jeans, but by growing into the woman you were designed to be with support from above and around you.

If you find a chapter that doesn't apply to you, feel free to skip on ahead, but I really recommend you read on through it. You might find something you now see differently because motherhood is ever changing. Maybe your friend or sister is in a different motherhood boat than you are. We all know the truth: the minute we think we've got a milestone or phase handled, our little darlings change the rules of the game. Good thing we love them more than life.

Happy reading!

Love,

Meredith

SECTION ONE:

UNIVERSAL INSECURITIES

CHAPTER 1

INSECURITIES ABOUT PREGNANCY AND BIRTH

———

"Making the decision to get pregnant is momentous. It is to decide forever to have your heart go walking around outside of your body."

—*ELIZABETH STONE*

"First comes love, then comes marriage, then comes the baby in the baby carriage." It's a simple nursery rhyme we joked about in second grade. Well, it is for some of us. I grew up going to Catholic school. I was taught sex education by a nun who took a vow of celibacy, so I assume she didn't have all that much experience to back up her claims.

Most of us girls go through adolescence convinced that looking at a penis will pretty much get you pregnant. It isn't until we stand of the ledge of parenthood that maybe this whole making a baby thing isn't quite as easy as the teenage scare tactics led us to believe.

Upon staring at the egg icon on my fertility app, I realized—even as a college-educated nurse—I still didn't know much about the whole conception process. I was blissfully ignorant that the decision to have a baby was simply deciding to have one, doing the deed, and poof! Two pink lines on a pregnancy test. Sure, I had a vague understanding of ovulation, had even heard the phrase "luteal phase," but I did not have much in the way of practical knowledge. My generation of women spends so much time trying to *not* get pregnant before we are ready, we don't focus on the actual statistics. The American Pregnancy Association provides the following statistics regarding couples actively trying to conceive unaided by medication or medical intervention:

- 30 percent get pregnant within the first cycle (about one month).
- 60 percent get pregnant within three cycles (about three months).
- 80 percent get pregnant within six cycles (about six months).
- 85 percent get pregnant within 12 cycles (about one year).
- 92 percent get pregnant within 48 cycles (about four years).

For the modern woman trying to conceive a child, it is easiest to do so naturally in her twenties. Fertility begins to decline with age, but there is a plethora of modern medical advances that make building a family possible later in life. This is not to say waiting to start a family is without potential risk; a healthy thirty-year-old has about a 20 percent chance of getting pregnant each month, but by age forty, there is only about a 5 percent chance. By age forty-five, very few women get pregnant naturally.

But what about when the family we desire doesn't go according to plan?

When not just the birthing process isn't what you envisioned but the whole getting pregnant, to begin with, takes more time, energy, and possibly medical intervention? The Center for Disease Control defines infertility as the inability to naturally conceive a child after one year of unprotected sex. But those who have struggled know it as something else entirely: "A terrible club with really great members."

Infertility isn't a part of my personal story, but because it does affect one in eight women, I would be remiss if I didn't include it. Because I cannot share my own experience, I turned to expert Sue Johnston, author of *Detours: Unexpected Journeys of Hope Conceived from Infertility* and an international member of RESOLVE: The National Infertility Association. She was kind enough to share her ten-year battle with infertility with me during our talk.

Sue painted a picture of her infertility journey that had me in tears. Even twenty-something years later, she still tells of each failed embryo transfer and describes the feeling of loss so vividly. Her husband, a career naval officer, had to transfer all over the world while she was undergoing invasive and hormone-altering treatments to begin their family. My favorite moment was when she told me about finally, finally expecting their only son. "We put on 'Son of a Son of a Sailor,' you know, the Jimmy Buffet song. Even though we didn't know he'd be a boy, we were expecting the third generation of Navy. And we danced in the kitchen singing." This image of joy after so much waiting made my heart swell. Sue now uses her experience and platform to inspire other women on their journey through infertility.

I don't personally have experience with infertility, but I do have experience with loss. Often pregnancy loss is deeply personal, and mothers are hesitant to share. The experience may come with a mixed bag of emotions such as guilt, grief, or even relief. Women may wonder if they could have done something differently. Had she known she was pregnant, she would have come off a medication or wouldn't have had that glass of wine. However, most of the time, miscarriage occurs when there's a genetic issue with the developing fetus. A healthy term fetus may never have been in the cards from conception.

Miscarriage is defined as the loss of a pregnancy before twenty weeks, after which point the loss is considered a stillbirth. It occurs in one in four pregnancies and typically occurs early in the pregnancy. There's still a stigma attached to the loss of pregnancy. Even those with the best intentions do not know how to deal with loss, especially when it is less tangible like a miscarriage.

When talking with other mothers, the moment you open up about miscarriage, you learn that everyone has a unique story to tell. One of the hardest parts of pregnancy loss, particularly early loss, is when few others know about the pregnancy. Sharing the information in whatever capacity you find comforting can help those feelings of isolation.

I had a miscarriage before I was pregnant with my oldest. That pregnancy was unique in that it was what's called a "missed miscarriage." The typical perception of a miscarriage is that you'll begin bleeding and subsequently go to the doctor, who finds an absent heartbeat.

I went in for my initial pregnancy appointment at eight weeks. I knew from the moment I took a pregnancy test that something felt off about this, but I'd convinced myself that this was simply because I'd never been pregnant before. It was hard to put my finger on exactly what felt *not quite right* to me. (Maybe moms really do have a sixth sense.) My symptoms of early pregnancy were there, yet vague. Nothing like I would later experience with healthy pregnancies.

The nurse practitioner caring for me recognized my anxiety. Although it wasn't typical for this practice to do ultrasounds at the confirmation appointment, she sent me across the hall to get one.

Scanning showed there was no development of the fetus, even though I should have been much further along according to my dates. They didn't have to tell me that something was wrong. I knew. I Googled enough pictures to know what it should look like. When the expected image wasn't present on the screen before me, the ultrasound tech said, "I'll be right back with the doctor" and she averted her gaze from me. I knew for sure. The piece of me that wanted to believe I'd been wrong, that I was just nervous, collapsed. I broke down. I had imagined myself being a mother since I was a little girl carrying around baby dolls. That moment will stick with me for the rest of my life: seeing what I had imagined and what I'd wanted so badly absent on the screen.

I felt like I had done something wrong and caused this to happen, or that God was telling me I wasn't supposed to be a mother because I lacked something. I cycled through questions, trying to figure out *Why me? Why did this happen to me?* Even though I knew I wasn't unique, it still felt very deeply personal.

I regret not being more supportive to my husband as I was wrapped in my grief. He had lost a baby too, though it's a different experience when it's not your body. I did not see or share his emotions through the process; I was stuck in my own grief. After that, I became a bit obsessed with the idea of having another baby to fix the loss I experienced.

I wanted so badly to not feel the hurt and loss. I thought replacing it with another child would make everything better. It would just heal the wound quickly, and that would be the end of it. What I didn't expect was the fear that would then overshadow every subsequent pregnancy. I was just waiting for the other shoe to drop. My innocence of pregnancy—the natural joy I'd expected—was tainted.

I also didn't expect that, while pregnant with my son, the due date for my first pregnancy would come up on the calendar, and it would be a very emotional day for me. I thought, *I'm pregnant with another baby, so it shouldn't affect me,* but I remembered the date. I think I always will.

Not everyone's fertility journey looks the same. Many women conceive before they are ready or when they are no longer planning to add to their families, which can be a huge source of stress or conflict between partners. It is very important to me to shed light on the issues of infertility and pregnancy loss, but that doesn't mean that we can't hold space for other kinds of difficulties.

If you are reading this book, I hope there is an end to your fertility journey that looks as you hope it will. I am very happy to say I now have two beautiful children. Birthing each of them was very different.

For my oldest, I felt very uninformed (mostly my fault for skipping all the actual birthing chapters in the baby books), overwhelmed, and as if I was not at all the main character in the story. Things happened. Interventions occurred maybe for my benefit or maybe not.

My second birth, a scheduled induction, was a much smoother experience, not because we picked a date, but because I was ready. I didn't plan out a playlist or have a seventeen-page birth plan (it had always been "a healthy baby and a healthy me"), but I was confident. Well, until my daughter was crowning, and I looked at my husband and said, "I cannot have two kids."

"A little late for that, babe," he replied.

There are thousands of blog posts, hundreds of books on "the way" to birth, different methods of hypnotherapy and relaxation, of pain control, of positioning, and more. Men and women who are far more learned than me have written monuments to the birthing process. One of my personal favorites though is Emily Oster's *Expecting Better*. In her book, Oster compiles mounds of relevant data regarding choices in birthing and then draws her own conclusions on common arguments. According to Oster, maybe all those taboo pregnancy foods are actually not so forbidden. She and I certainly don't agree on everything, but you'd be hard pressed to find two women who do totally agree in motherhood.

I am a nurse married to a doctor. We are pretty entrenched in the idea of medical intervention, so we knew hospital births were for us. I had no way to predict if I would be one of the moms that ended up with an emergency C-section or twenty-minute labor. Although we want to perfectly predict what childbirth will be like to help us prepare for parenthood, most of these predictions are out of our control. I'm not saying we can't be informed—or as my sister-in-law says, "the heroines of our own birth stories," which sounds a lot better than how I felt after three hours of pushing—but we do have to make a plan and then surrender.

I can't tell you how many times I hear moms telling birth stories including things like the following:

"But I had an epidural..."

"But I had a C-section..."

As if they need the preposition qualifier. **You brought a baby into this world. You are amazing. Period. End of story.**

Our motherhood stories never look like a single, linear, cookie-cutter journey. The wandering, the mistakes, the everyday moments are what make up our lives with our littles. We wouldn't trade them for someone else's idea of perfection any day. If you glean nothing else from this book, know this: **by being a mother you are amazing, plain and simple.** You were made for that baby and that baby for you, however long it took them to get here and by whatever means they entered the world.

"Travis," I said. "I think my water just broke."

He looked at me sleepily and said, "You probably just peed. Don't be embarrassed. It happens to pregnant women."

There we were, thirty minutes after my husband's return from work at the hospital, loading up to drive back. I was wearing a bulky adult diaper I had ordered online after obsessively googling, and my husband had traded his after-work drink for a cup of coffee. We only pulled back in the driveway three times for him to separately acquire a phone charger (I had two packed in my bag along with fifty other things I wouldn't use).

I had been convinced for weeks that my water was going to break rom-com style in some extremely mortifying public place. Why was I so sure when roughly only 15 percent of amniotic sacs rupture prior to labor? Call it my first bit of mother's intuition, when in fact it was likely just my anxiety showing. I slept on a towel for weeks, having no idea how much "water" was all up in there. I sat on a beach towel to watch tv. I was sure it would happen. I count this as one of the only times I have predicted an outcome in motherhood.

And that's what it was: ninety minutes of pushing to get my sweet boy out. Oxygen on my face, I stared down in the perfect pink squish that was my freshly birthed son. I heard one nurse say to the other, "Do you have the baby's chart?" What? He has his own chart. That means he's *really* his own separate person from me. This is a realization I had that continues to happen again and again and again. My kids are not just an extension of me.

From the moment you decide to start a family, the reality of the motherhood journey may not look like your expectations. If there is loss or infertility in your history, you are not alone. If you have not experienced loss or infertility personally, you surely know someone who has. But you also likely know what it is to stare down at a perfect smattering of eyelashes and, with a lump in your throat, read,

"On the night you were born,

the moon smiled with such wonder

that the stars peeked in to see you

and the night wind whispered,

'Life will never be the same.'"

—Nancy Tillman, *On the Night You Were Born*

CHAPTER 2

INSECURITIES ABOUT FEEDING OUR CHILDREN

———

"Much of what we learn about eating comes from the way our parents feed us."

—BEE WILSON, *FIRST BITE: HOW WE LEARN TO EAT*

Admittedly, breastfeeding my first child wasn't something I loved, but we made it through to what my self-critical mommy mind deemed a respectable eight months and three days. No, it's not the actual length of time that I was critical about— because honestly who cares. What I was obsessed with was making sure both of my kids got EXACTLY eight months and three days so future me didn't have to wonder if one kid developed asthma or fell behind on a milestone because he or she missed out on thirty-six hours of breastmilk. How's that for very accurate insight into my inner mommy monologue?

Breastfeeding my first was full of typical challenges, like wondering what I could wear to ensure a Janet Jackson half-time moment at any time in any place? The issues morphed with my second child. Gone were the days of *Friends* reruns while

I nursed and nursed and nursed and snacked and snacked. I was still expected to parent while actively feeding. Many people think bottle feeding is easier, but I vehemently disagree. Feeding an infant is a ton of work no matter how you do it. Add a toddler into the mix, and you deserve a medal.

During my very first day alone with both of my children sans the aid of my husband or mother, I decided to rock it. The thought of an open day with two mini people to keep alive scared me, so I jammed our schedule. My kids are eighteen months apart. Yes, it was planned that way, despite what some hopefully well-meaning strangers have asked.

Two birthday parties. An expertly timed grocery pickup. Easy, toddler-friendly dinner. I even planned to enjoy a glass of wine after they were both sleeping. I was super mom.

Anyone could see that my sleep-deprived soul was slightly too ambitious. The day didn't go quite according to plan. Even though, somewhere deep in the recesses of my brain, I knew this plan might be a bit much with a ten-day-old and a nine-teen-month-old, I was determined. And Hell hath no fury like a tired mother's scorn.

8:10 a.m. Fueled by coffee and adrenaline, I set off with my kids to "Pancakes and Pajamas," the first party of the day. Two of the three of us cried on the way there, *but not me.* Tears did burn my eyes, however, when I tried to pull my swollen fourth trimester body into pre-baby jeans, but that's what yoga pants are for. After a game of arm Tetris, I maneuvered a carrier, a toddler, a gift, and some dignity out of the car. I smiled and nodded at all the moms in skinny jeans and booties while I looked like I'd been through a suburban version of war, politely refusing to let anyone hold my baby because *germs.*

9:15 a.m. Time for my tiny to eat. If you have ever nursed a tiny baby, you know that to quick latch discretely takes a bit of practice. In the beginning, everyone is half naked. I asked another mom to keep an eye on my oldest while I positioned myself in a back room to feed my daughter. Yes, early nursing does sometimes feel akin to a "nipple cheese grater" as Andrea Jansen describes in her TEDx Talk, "The Perfect Mother Needs to Go." But this was not right. I felt glass shards, burning pain. I looked down to see red streaking creeping its way up my chest. I didn't think this was the glass ceiling I was supposed to shatter as a millennial woman.

Deep breaths. No big deal. I can handle this.

10:00 a.m. Party Number One drew to a close. The children were jealous of the birthday kid's new toys, and parents were pretending they really did want to spend their Saturday morning making chit chat with friends of friends. After loading up my kids, I did a quick search of my favorite breastfeeding site to figure out what might be going on. Clogged ducts popped up on KellyMom.com.

Of course, I thought. *No big deal. I just had to pump. Fine, I had two hours between parties. I had this under control.*

1:00 p.m. Fast forward through Party Number Two, which was a bit of a blur as I started feeling really not so great. Probably the stress. Probably the lack of sleep. On to my grocery pick up.

3:45 p.m. Seventy-six minutes later, everyone was crying—my newborn from what could only be an epic diaper situation and my toddler because who likes to sit in the car for over an hour? And I was crying because, well, see all of the above. I changed and nursed the baby, noticing the streaking on my chest had reached farther up. I gave my toddler my phone out of desperation, judging myself for being *that* mom. Spoiler alert: three years later, I embrace being that mom.

4:45 p.m. Cue the arrival of my not-so-friendly grocery deliverer. He leaned into my car to notice everyone crying only to say to me, "I'm sure what's going on in here can't be that bad."

Cool dude, I thought. *I'm holding it together by a nursing bra strap and a prayer.* Finally loaded up with half of my original order of groceries (a fun nugget of information I would discover upon arriving home), we were off.

The trio of tears continued until bedtime when both babes were fluffed, buffed, and asleep.

8:30 p.m. *Geez,* I thought. *I feel like absolute crap.* The thermometer blinking 102.1 made sense of that realization. Medicine, a call to the after-hours line, and some really pathetic texts to my husband later, I found myself with a formal diagnosis of mastitis and some antibiotics waiting at the pharmacy.

For those who aren't familiar, mastitis and plugged ducts are the two most common breastfeeding complications. Per Kelly-Mom, one of the leading online support networks for nursing mothers, both conditions are caused by milk stasis, or clogged milk. In the case of a plugged duct, one of the nipple pores (yes, it comes out of more than one place) gets clogged, kind of like a pimple. As the milk thickens in the clogged pore, a lump forms behind the clog due to inability to empty the "pipe." Mastitis is similar, only that clogged duct has crossed over to an infectious process. Signs like fever, chills, red streaking, and the tell-tale lump in the affected breast signal that there is something wrong.

If you're considering breastfeeding and have yet to experience it, you might be thinking, "All this fun plus the potential for cracked and bleeding nipples? Cool, sign me up for that *and* stepping barefoot on Legos!" But with antibiotics (if you have full blown mastitis), hot showers/compresses, pressure from the base of the breast toward the nipple, it's a situation that can be remedied rather quickly.

Many parents choose bottle-feeding due to anatomical or personal preference, to share care of the baby amongst both parents, or for a host of other reasons. If you look at longitudinal studies of babies over time, the "breast is best" argument doesn't have quite as big of a leg to stand on as many would have you believe. Rumors be damned, formula is safe. It's not a guarantee of childhood obesity or poor test scores—sibling studies prove that to be untrue. The data, as is often the case, was correlation rather than causation. According to a study by Colen and Ramey, breastfed infants performed better than bottle-fed infants on ten out of eleven markers, until they compared siblings. Upon further examination, factors such as socioeconomic status (which likely allowed breastfeeding in the first place) accounted for the disparity, rather than the actual feeding method.

I am certainly an advocate for breastfeeding. After all, I am a former pediatric intensive care unit nurse. The American Academy of Pediatrics recommends exclusive breastfeeding for the first six months of life. But I also recommend, and so I imagine would any pediatrician, if and when it works for the mother *and* the child **both** or it's not working. One reason many women choose to breastfeed is the cost. Free sounds pretty good. But is it really free? Many women don't have the time currency to devote to breastfeeding or pumping. The choice to breastfeed was right for me—for a time. Eventually, I was *done!* But it is not right or possible for everyone.

In motherhood there are a lot of situations that are "You do you." This is one of them. It's not a safety issue. I don't say this to take away from the experience if it is what is right for you and your family. I have had beautiful moments in the middle of the night nursing my babies, but if the sickest babies in the NICU can get formula, then yours can too, and they can still grow to be healthy, strong, and smart. This is very much a "You do you" moment, Mama.

So, what happens after the "bottle, the boob, or both" debate? You're totally in the clear on feeling judged internally or externally by how your child eats, right? Maybe not. The conversation just shifts. Although I am a proponent of kids eating what everyone else is eating, I am lucky that my two kids generally are not picky eaters. But I can assure you that all families struggle with *something*. No mama is immune to kids refusing to eat or throwing food on the floor. If you struggle with mealtime in your house, you are not alone.

According to Mascola, Bryson, and Agras, a 2010 study in *Eating Behaviors,* shows that out of one hundred and twenty children (between two and eleven years of age), up to 22 percent were picky eaters. They also asserted that these picky eating habits produced parental anxiety. And of course, they did! People constantly comment on how kids eat. As parents, we tend to take comments like that—positive or negative—as a reflection of us when in fact they don't mean anything at all.

I sat down with registered dietician Diana Rice to talk about the role of nutrition in our kids' lives as infants and across the lifespan. Diana started her career in journalism working for women's magazines, where she saw firsthand just how often the topic of health appeared in such publications. Now a married mom of two daughters, she follows intuitive eating and health for all body sizes philosophies; this is in accordance with Carbonneau et al's 2017 study, which states, "Health at Every Size® (HAES®) interventions focus on healthy lifestyle by promoting behavioral changes related to diet and physical activity, while emphasizing self-acceptance and well-being through an empowerment and intuitive approach." In speaking with Diana, I realized how our upbringings impact the way we introduce and exemplify food relationships to our children.

Diana shared with me something I have wondered about before but could not articulate in the way that she could. "Kids are learning to eat the same way they're learning to read," she said. "We have these expectations of them just loving to eat sushi and bento boxes, and if your kid isn't doing that, there's something wrong with you as a parent. Additionally, your child is normal because, one, they're just a developmentally appropriate kid, or two, they may have sensory challenges." Acknowledging the incredible challenge of sensory or avoidant restrictive food intake disorders—a severe form of picky eating now classified as a full-fledged eating disorder—she went on to describe how we seem to accept adults with a distaste for a food or dislike of a texture; however, for children who do the same, we want a label, a diagnosis. Similarly, we want children who always behave and are pleasant when we, as adults, often have moody, difficult days.

Diana and I talked about the difference between the Wonder Bread sandwiches with absent crusts of our youth in contrast to the rainbow bento boxes our children are accustomed to. As we spoke, I realized how we unnecessarily complicate feeding our kids. She told me about touring a daycare for her oldest daughter, and how, upon finding out she was a registered dietician, the daycare immediately defended the corn dogs served for lunch that day, adding that fruit was also served. She laughed and told them that corndogs were a perfectly normal food for a kid to eat.

I love her stance that all food serves a purpose. I think about my own flawed relationship with food and how if you tell me I can't have chocolate, then that's the only thing I'll want. Well, turns out our kids are human too. Making certain foods forbidden can have the unintended consequence of causing negative self-thoughts in our children. If treats are "bad," are our kids "bad" for wanting them?

I am certainly guilty of calling myself "bad" for food indulgences. In nearly every moms' group I attend, I hear both, "How do I make my child a better eater?" and, at the same time, "How do I lose weight?" Our kids pick up on our dietary restrictions. Are we going to mess this up? Of course. I do it all the time.

But recognition that we are holding these two truths at the same time may be the first step. Let's take the pressure off ourselves and our kiddos so that they have the best chance of developing healthy eating patterns (more on mamas and body image later). Breastfed or bottle-fed, most of our kids are going to grow up at one point or another preferring mac 'n' cheese to zucchini—I know I do. Our job is to make sure they have exposure to all the amazing foods our world has to offer.

CHAPTER 3

INSECURITIES ABOUT HOW OUR KIDS SLEEP

———

"Sleep when the baby sleeps. Should I also clean when the baby cleans?"

—CREDIT UNKNOWN

When I was a relatively new nurse, I was working night shift. It was about three o'clock in the morning, and I only had one patient, which meant I was open for admission as a typical assignment is to ICU patients. The charge nurse called to tell me I'd be admitting a three-week-old infant who was found unresponsive.

The more seasoned nurses all looked at each other and said, "Rollover." I figured they were talking about a traffic accident. Of course, I knew about safe sleep practices from my training in nursing school, but I had yet to learn what they all seemed to know about the otherwise healthy baby admitted in the middle of the night.

An accidental death occurred because the mother had smothered her own child. Statistically, this kind of event is rare.

I prepped the room, making sure I had all my lines, my resuscitation drugs drawn up in tiny syringes based on the age and weight of my incoming patient. I prepped the blankets, the warmer, everything I would need as the patient was receiving CPR en route to the hospital.

How could this happen?

Now, as a mother, I know exactly how it happens. We are exhausted. We are stretched thin. We are told to exclusively breastfeed. But you can't pump and then bottle feed getting only forty-five minute stretches of sleep. We are indoctrinated to believe that self-sufficiency is a prize more precious than gold and asking for help is for the weak—for the *bad* mothers.

What happened next was a blur of what felt like hundreds of hands. Helping. Assisting. Pumping. Pulling. Working to save that baby.

All for naught. What I heard next was a sound that will echo in my head for the rest of my life. One of the most agonizing sounds I've ever heard.

The mother's wail.

Of course, I'd lost patients before and have lost patients since; the sound of a mother mourning the loss of her child is always gut wrenching.

But this mother, even in this accident, knew this moment could have been prevented.

I'll admit full stop that I probably have some level of PTSD from this event that I carried with me through the birth of my children. As I said, statistically this kind of thing does not happen often. I know that plenty of people who love their children co-sleep and never have an adverse event occur. But having gone through the experience that I did, I went out of my way to ensure that that wouldn't happen to me. I read what seemed like thousands of blog posts on safe sleep. I researched all the baby products I would use and did some deep internet dives into how their "safety" is determined.

I, admittedly and shamefully, was judgmental about other people who weren't as passionate about safe sleep as I was. I'm horrified to admit that because no one has ever changed their mind based on the harsh judgment of someone else; compassion, support and information may shift someone's actions, but never judgment.

There are lots of moments in motherhood that are "You do you," but sleep isn't one of those for me. Remember that we all bring certain experiences from our own childhoods and early adulthoods into parenthood, which influences how we parent. Out partners do the same. And as I have admitted, I feel very strongly about sleep safety. Surely my conviction is shaped by the experiences I had in the pediatric ICU that night.

The American Academy of Pediatrics, the holy grail of advice on kids' safety, states that kids should sleep according to the ABCs. "A" stands for "alone," "B" for "on their backs," and "C" for "in a crib" (bassinets and play yards also meet the safety criteria) with no pillows, stuffed animals, blankets, or crib bumpers. Swaddling is encouraged until eight-weeks-old or until the baby can independently roll—whichever comes first.

This is likely nothing like how you or I were put to sleep as infants: on our bellies, in frilly cribs, and with stuffed bears. In the 1990s, the Back to Sleep campaign started and dropped infant death rates by greater than 50 percent. This changed the norm in the US of putting babies to sleep on their stomachs to putting them down on their backs. The old school of thought was that stomach sleeping was safer than other positions if an infant were to spit up while sleeping—keeping them from aspirating. Based on this study, we now know that babies are more at risk breathing recirculated air, suffering positional asphyxiation (collapse of airway from sleeping at an angle), or suffocating from an object, like a crib bumper.

What about bed-sharing and sleep positioners? Can they be used safely? When I look at the data, I am inclined to say no. Yes, people do bed-share (often called co-sleeping) and have no adverse events occur, but the risks are much higher than if you avoid it altogether. In my opinion, this is survivor's confirmation bias. Do I think these people are terrible mothers? Absolutely not. I think we are all flipping tired.

From the mothers I have talked to who choose to co-sleep, the most common answers I get are the following:

"I feel safer with my baby closer."

"It's easier to breastfeed."

"That's how my family always did it."

We are given information that contradicts other information, and many of us without support networks are just trying to get by. Even though I can wholeheartedly put myself back into the mindset of sleep deprivation and fear, with my nursing background and utter awe of what the American Academy of Pediatrics has done for kids, I cannot condone any form of bed-sharing or unsafe sleep. I believe it to be unsafe and not at all worth the risk.

I recognize this is a very strong stance on the subject.

It is entirely possible that with a different personality type I could have had that exact same experience and been much more laissez-faire in the sleep department. Instead, pregnant with my first child, I poured myself into the wide world of parenting advice on the internet—which is akin to Alice and that hole she tumbles down. First came *Babywise*, a classic book on how to make your kid sleep when you want them to. It was a total failure for me. Not only could I not make the schedule work, but I also then gained more anxiety from getting anxious about the schedule not working. Did you follow that? Yep, not for me.

My sweet spot was learning about age-appropriate wake times. Suddenly, my baby actually fell asleep for naps. It was glorious. That is, until the dreaded four-month sleep regression. For those of you not familiar, around four months, babies begin to alter their sleep patterns and have more difficulty falling asleep on their own. Basically, it highlights whatever crutches they have been using thus far—most of which are totally age-appropriate and normal—and increases your Starbucks spending.

Around this time, I began my foray into the wide world of sleep training. Many mamas are scared of this concept as it doesn't feel natural to them, or they think it involves abandoning your baby to scream bloody murder for hours on end. I sat down with sleep consultant Abby Sharpe to discuss her knowledge on the subject. "We teach our children how to eat, how to ride a bike, how to do almost everything," Abby shared. "Why would we expect that sleep would be any different?"

Abby is mom to three boys, and she worked diligently at sleep training all three. After observing the differences in behavior between children close to her who were sleep trained and those who were not, she claims that there is a method for everyone. Combating the widely held ideas that sleep training is a black and white subject, Abby suggests that if what you are doing is working for you, then you have no need for her services. Conversely, if you and your child are suffering, it's time for gentle intervention.

Like almost every interview I have done for this book with a seasoned mother, her wisdom spilled over beyond my original questions. When I asked her about the most common issue facing parents regarding sleep, she simply answered, "Anxiety." She went on to describe that we all are just doing the best we can. "We frankly are given more instructions to care for a succulent than for a newborn, so of course we are terrified we'll mess up." We both dove down the rabbit hole of conflicting information on the internet that can make parental anxiety, particularly when combined with a string of sleepless nights, all the worse.

Abby asserts that a well-rested child and family functions better and, in more harmony, than those who lose sleep. I tend to agree. Although my kids are far from perfect sleepers—just check under my eyes for confirmation—we are much better for the structure I have tried to impart. Minimal crying involved—on their part.

For those of you who likely don't have some scarring sleep-related memory to shape your experiences regarding motherhood and sleep, I am sure we can agree on one universal truth of parenthood: we are tired.

So, what can we do to get more sleep safely? Let's look to the experts. One of my favorite resources for healthy sleeping guidelines is the book *The Happy Sleeper*. In this text, licensed psychotherapists, Heather Turgeon and Julie Wright use a common sense approach combined with science to help parents combat the most common sleep-related problems. Some of their recommended methods are night waking, early morning waking, and learning to sleep independently.

Gathered from my own experience, *The Happy Sleeper*, and some other books on sleep in light of the American Academy of Pediatrics guidelines, here are some things to try if you are up a sleep creek:

- Utilize white noise. (The static sound mimics the sounds babies hear in the womb.)
- Create a bedtime routine that is short and predictable. (This allows baby to know that sleep is coming.)
- Swaddle or use a sleep sack depending on the baby's age.
- Follow safe sleep practices like placing the babe alone, on their back, and in a crib or approved sleep space, like a bassinet or play yard. (This is often called the ABCs— Alone, Back, and Crib—of sleep.)
- Don't buy expensive sleep gadgets. (Babies have slept without them forever. Save your money and your sanity.)
- Try putting a heating pad in the baby's sleep space and removing it before placing them down. (This will warm up their sleep environment.)
- If your baby keeps waking up, gently pick them up and keep repeating until they self-settle. (Use the pick up, put down method for babies who are too young to formally sleep train.)
- Ask for help. Martyrs don't make good mothers.

The number one question I was asked as a new mother was how the baby was sleeping. Everyone had something to say about it. I never felt I could answer honestly. If you are struggling, answer honestly. Wake your partner up. Ask for help. Reach out. If you know a new mother, go and hold her baby so she can take a nap. Don't be surprised when she turns you down, though. Our conditioning to do it all runs deep.

CHAPTER 4

INSECURITIES ABOUT OUR PARENTING STYLES

"Children are educated by what the grown-up is and not by his talk."

—CARL JUNG

I stood in a church gym with dozens of pairs of moms and tots. My own little boy clung to the plastic airplane toy he'd chosen for Bring a Toy to Share Day. As soon as he realized there were in fact other toys—some of them brighter, shinier, and louder than his—the shyness melted into excitement. Upon approaching another mom, her son roughly the same age as my little, he reached out to grab the child's plastic shopping cart. The mom quickly pulled the toy away and stated matter-of-factly to me, "We aren't sharing today."

Ummm, what?

The whole point of these shindigs is to teach people skills to our little people. I picked up my son and turned on my heel in a wave of confusion and, to be honest, judgement. *Who doesn't make their kid share? Isn't that like the cardinal rule of childhood interaction? Sharing is caring.*

At the time, I did what I knew to do when I felt in over my head with parenting. I wrote a blog post. I called it "Why My Kid Has to Share and Yours Should Too." Honestly, it did not go over that well. I had a lot of comments from moms about how sharing was akin to sexual assault. Yes, you read that correctly.

"If you ask my daughter to share her Barbie, it's the same as making her give you her body."

"My son will share if he feels like it."

Asking a child to share was taking something that was theirs and forcing it away from them. Ladies, welcome to the wide world of helicopter parenting.

I fully recognize the difference between asking two kids to take turns (which is what I meant by "sharing") and having a child come in and take whatever they want only to have the behavior defended as "sharing." Of course, there are exceptions, like security blankets. It's a parent's responsibility to teach young children that bringing a flashy toy to wave in front of other kids only to say, "It's special, and I'm not sharing." is asking for a teeny tiny *West Side Story* in the sandbox. Sadly, as a culture, we have moved into this realm where concepts as fundamental as sharing are overshadowed by aggression and defensiveness.

Middle ground does exist between the two extremes of raising mini-narcissists and forcing children to give up their toys. According to Heather Shumaker on the Positive Parenting Solutions blog, forcing kids to share makes them feel taken advantage of. Conversely, she recommends teaching your child to say, "You can have this when I am finished," which is a great compromise.

Most people parenting today were parented differently than they choose for their own children. Glennon Doyle exemplifies how parenting has changed throughout the past few generations in her bestseller, *Untamed*:

"Every generation of parents receives a memo when they leave the hospital with their baby.

My grandmother's memo:

Here is the baby. Take it home and let it grow. Let it speak when spoken to. Carry on with your lives.

My mother's memo: Here is your baby. Take her home and then get together each day with your friends who also have these things. Drink Tab before four o'clock and wine coolers after. Smoke cigarettes and play cards. Lock the kids out of the house and let them in only to eat and sleep.

Lucky bastards."

Sounds just like parenting today, where from the beginning you are doing everything wrong if your whole life isn't devoted to making sure your child never experiences so much as a paper cut. Maybe it's the widespread availability of birth control, or maybe it's many of us waiting until later in life to have babies, but with parenting styles vastly shifting, many of us are flying blind.

I talked to Aly Frei, Director of Becoming Parents, a program designed to help couples navigate the journey into parenthood together through resources, workshops, and integrated support. Per the Becoming Parents website, the program "focuses on reducing the predictable challenges of new parenthood by strengthening the couple's resilience, promoting self-care and community support, and bringing research about infant communication and development directly to parents." I particularly enjoy the emphasis on fatherhood in the program. Sure, I personally write about motherhood—don't really have all that much experience as a dad. But I love the focus on the integral role dads play in the lives of children and what an impact babies have on relationships. As Aly shared with me, "There is not a single relationship that stays the same when you add a baby into the mix."

Candid, competent, and kind, Aly entertained me by describing her own parenting journey. As a Seattle-based mom of two, Aly described some of the resources available in her area, but even though she knew the benefits of these resources, it was still hard for her to take advantage of them. Aly and I talked at length about the different styles of parenting and about how just having an ideal doesn't mean you will always land there.

With her client's permission, Aly shared with me an anecdote of a client named Meghan and her young child. Meghan's daughter had a particular habit, as babies do, of waking up at an ungodly hour every day. So rather than always rising with her and being less than her best Mom self, Meghan would transfer her baby, Esme, to the Pack 'n Play by the window each morning. Esme was safe, happy, and getting some Vitamin D. Meghan had the slightest thought that she should get up with Esme, but that was quickly forgotten in place of her much needed extra down time—until they had house guests.

One morning following her typical routine, Esme lay in the light of the window happily playing when Meghan found her house guest staring at her, asking, "Do you always just leave her here *alone*?"

Aly went on to describe that while Meghan knew Esme was safe and happy, the judgement of another, even while well intentioned, made her question her methods. Help over judgement is paramount in parenting. Aly went on to share, "I teach people how to be parents for a living, and I've had moments where I felt like didn't know what I was doing. And the truth is we all need help. All of us need a community, but those of us with child rearing or health backgrounds may be even more hesitant to seek it out." This sentiment felt so true to me. As a pediatric nurse, I was certain I had everything under control for my kids. After all, who was better qualified? I believe each of us is the best mama for our own babies, but we all need some help.

Many of us turn to experts when deciding how to parent our minis. There are thousands of books out there to make you feel like you're failing. Or is that just me? Every time I read a parenting book, it seems everything I am doing is going to land my kid squarely in serial killer territory. Okay, maybe it's not that bad, but I digress.

Our culture is so obsessed with the idea of fitting into a mold that we like to label everything, including parenting styles. While the majority of us are probably a mixed bag of styles, most books take one extreme stance or another.

I struggle a lot with the rise of positive parenting but not because I think it's a bad idea. Positive parenting is defined in the literature review by Seay et al. (2014) as "the continual relationship of a parent(s) and a child or children that includes caring, teaching, leading, communicating, and providing for the needs of a child consistently and unconditionally." Sounds like a great idea!

It is a wonderful concept, especially for all of us who were more than likely raised in the '80s and '90s, when authoritarian parenting ruled the land. However, I often see gentle parenting or positive parenting turn into permissive parenting, which isn't good for anyone.

The original philosophy of attachment parenting was derived in the 1960s as a way to nurture positive relationships between mothers and children. The term currently means something entirely different. In 1993, Dr. Sears capitalized on the term "attachment parenting," moving it from the sphere of authoritative parenting (loving with safe boundaries) into the sphere of permissive parenting (where the child's needs surpass those of the adult). I know I will likely ruffle some feathers with this opinion, but I do not believe children should lead. It is our job to set firm, clear boundaries for our kids and to do so in a loving manner.

Now, before I deconstruct entire parenting dynamics without any sort of sociology or psych degree, I'm going to throw a few other things at you. In my opinion, no parent or child is going to fit perfectly into any framework; every single theory has one contradiction or two nuances that aren't going to work for each family because each child and parent is different.

In my generation, parents didn't apologize to kids when they messed up. This is no dig at my actual parents, who are wonderful humans. You either fell into one of two categories: the parent or the child. Parents had this omniscient knowledge of the world that made them so different from us. I do feel like that is shifting in the culture, reflecting in this ability to apologize to your kids when you do something wrong—to show them how to make a mistake and make amends.

It is my theory that the rise of child-led parenting is a response to the traumatic rigidity of our own childhoods, and some parents swing quite far into permissive territory. Now if you go the other side of the spectrum, you'll find authoritarian parenting, that is *all* boundaries—total rigidity of rules and parents as gatekeepers. So, where I try to land is somewhere in the middle, where you have a balance of boundaries and safety.

We know in all things from wine to Oreos, moderation is key, but it is also incredibly difficult. What parenting style you choose must fit you, your child, and your lifestyle. Oh, and here's a spoiler alert: those things are subject to change.

We need to look for our own implicit biases in parenting. Most of us are trying to do something different from how were raised, even if you had wonderful parents. And even if you think that your childhood was "perfect," you now likely have a partner who has his or her own set of ideals on what constitutes a healthy parent-child relationship.

When attempting to strike a balance between safety and positive expectations, authoritative parenting is ideal. For example, if you get too permissive, parents tend to be more like their child's friend. When I was a teenager and young adult, I loved the show *Gilmore Girls*. How cool would it be to have a mom who was your best friend like that? Now as a mother, I watch it and think, *What the heck was Lorelai thinking?* Then you have the "all safety and no boundaries approach." Boundaries are important for us to thrive as they help children feel safe in the world. I find that parents are often permissive but wish to label themselves as gentle or positive. I have no qualms with gentle parenting, other than that I personally struggle with the "calm" requirement of it.

Janet Lansbury is a wonderful example of a parenting expert who teaches respectful parenting. Essentially, she teaches the mom I wish I could be—all firm limits filled with love and no overreaction from the mother. Her podcast is called *Unruffled*, which is wonderful, but I am in fact often quite ruffled. For anyone interested in ideal how-to-mom lessons, I'd highly recommend her views. I would also add the caveat of knowing that everyone has bad days and teaching your children how to respond when they are struggling is important too.

With a perfectly behaved child, it is relatively easy to subscribe to a parenting style. As my childhood neighbor's mother used to say, "If I'd only been mother to my oldest, I'd have thought I was a gifted parent." But it turns out that our kids are actually tiny humans who have willpower and minds of their own, and perfect behavior just isn't going to happen most of the time because we're human. So, what do we do then?

One important thing to do is figure out what you do as a parent when you get stressed. This is a long, ongoing process and something I'm not super proud of, but I'm willing to admit that I go back to being authoritarian when I'm stressed. My Achilles' heel is yelling. I struggle when I feel like my kids aren't listening to me as normal, healthy kids do. The problem is that yelling never makes anyone feel any better. And after the storm of yelling comes the inevitable flood of #momguilt.

The flip side of this is that I have gotten an awful lot of chances to apologize to my kids. It teaches children that everyone has limits and people will lose their temper. If we live in a world where we're never allowed to get frustrated by something that someone else does, what is that going to teach our kids about the real world? People get mad or frustrated, especially if you don't follow through on commitments. Adults are imperfect people, and teaching kids that from a young age may help to combat some perfectionistic tendencies moving into adolescence.

I would imagine, though, that the ultimate goal is the same: to raise a good human who is self-sufficient and contributes positively to society. When I was pregnant with my first, I decided from the get-go that I was going to be really good at this raising-a-good-human thing.

I was going to never lose my temper. Why would I with a perfectly behaved child?

My kid would sleep twelve hours each night, with a two-hour nap during which I would tidy the house and bake something Julia Child-esque.

I would always know what to do in any situation, I was the adult after all.

My kids would never do or say (or repeat) something embarrassing I had done or said.

I would never have a kid with a perpetually runny nose. What kind of mother didn't carry those deck of cards-size tissues?

I would never under any circumstances give my kid a screen so I could have a breather, work out, clean, or eat cookies in the pantry.

Turns out, it's slightly more complicated than wishful thinking and lofty ideals.

CHAPTER 5

DEAR EVERYONE

Dear Breast Pump,

Why do you sound like you are saying "milk milkmaidddd" to me every time I turn you on? Is it you? Is it me? I am starting to feel judged.

Dear TikTok,

I don't understand you. I used to have a Myspace and an AIM away message. I may not be cool and use cry-laughing emojis like all other self-respecting millennials, but whatever. I have a 401k and don't drive a scooter.

Dear coworker,

I hope you enjoyed stealing my flavored coffee creamer every day this week out of the staff fridge. Joke's on you. It was pumped milk.

Dear husband's boss,

Thank you for arguing with me that I, in fact, was still pregnant when my baby was in the stroller next to me because I still "looked pregnant." You are an ass because you "look like one."

Dear sister-in-law,

Yes, I know that this is not how you burped your baby. I know because every single time I burp mine you remind me of that fact. And it's probably why my niece is now in the gifted and talented program—because of the way you burped her. Get over yourself. Burp.

Dear working mom neighbor,

No, I don't have a clean house because I "have nothing else to do." Do I ask you why you aren't the CEO because all you do is work? Mind your own business.

Dear stay-at-home mom friend,

Yes, I feel guilty when I have to miss my kids' activities, but not all the time. I am a good mom because I have a job that fulfills me.

Dear anti-vaxx cousin on Instagram,

Yes, my baby got her shots. No, she doesn't have a third arm and doesn't stick to the stainless steel fridge now. And no, I don't want to hear about your amazing business opportunity.

Dear husband's snoring,

It's getting really old to watch you sleep while I stay awake feeding our baby and plotting your death. I'm only joking. Maybe.

Dear crockpot,

I love you and how you shred all meat the same. You are the great equalizer.

Dear refrigerator repairman,

Yes. I am pregnant. Yes. Just one baby. No, you may not touch my belly. Yep. This is awkward.

Dear entire world,

Why are you commenting on the size of my bump?

Signed, every pregnant woman everywhere

Dear coworker,

Yes, I know my kids will be close in age together. Yes, I do know how this happens. Thanks for your awkward sex joke in the workplace.

Dear Trader Joe's,

Thank you for allowing me to be basic and feel healthy at the same time. I like having my foot planted squarely in two worlds.

Dear Susan,

Yes, I am so, so glad for you that you can make meals from scratch every night, but I am not sure my kids would like Hamachi Sriracha towers nightly; I happen to like frozen Dino Nuggets.

Dear meal trains,

It is super nice to get food delivered after having a baby/surgery/what have you, but can we make a rule that it is porch drop-off only? I don't want to talk to anyone/clean my house/let them hold my baby/put on pants. Cool?

Dear well-meaning old ladies at the grocery store,

Calling me fluffy is the same as calling me fat. It just means you think I resemble a stuffed animal. It's still mean—just awkward and mean. Keep your opinions and your tissue-stuffed sleeves away from my infant during flu season.

Dear inventor of mesh underwear,

I hope you have retired on a Caribbean beach somewhere because that idea is pure gold.

Yes, she's a girl. Yes, I'm sure.

Yes, that really is the name we chose. No, you cannot call him something else.

Yes, am I pregnant. No, I didn't just eat a big lunch. No, I am not pregnant. Yes, I am sure, I just had a big lunch.

I am smiling like this because the alternative is telling you that I actually don't give a crap about your opinion about my parenting.

Do you ever get halfway to where you are going and realize you've been listening to Baby Shark the whole time with empty car seats?

Dear boss,

I am sorry I said I had to go potty in the middle of the important Zoom meeting. I wear a lot of hats.

Dear dog,

I am sorry I used to give you more attention. I really do feel bad about it. Take this floor full of puffs as an apology.

Dear twenty-year-old me, who knew so much about being a good mom,

Shut up. You know nothing.

Dear parenting books,

You give me anxiety.

Dear hot tea and *Dateline*,

You are now my wild Friday night.

Dear fruit snacks,

You are toddler crack. I used to be above bribery. I also used to have abs.

Dear kids,

Go to bed so I can eat your snacks and watch serial killer documentaries.

Dear kids,

Wake up so I can cuddle you.

Dear time,

Speed up so they will grow up and out of this hard phase. Mommy is struggling.

Dear time,

Slow down—you are flying by too fast.

SECTION TWO:

WHY THEY EXIST: INTERNAL & EXTERNAL PRESSURES

CHAPTER 6

THE ROLE OF COMPARISON

———

"Even the mighty Sun might get depressed if He started comparing Himself with the moon: 'People take me for granted and sing praises of the moon.'"

—SHUNYA

Most of us can agree that 2020 may have been the weirdest year ever to be a parent. In the spring of 2020, when we were all fairly certain checking the mail was going to lead to a COVID hospitalization, I hopped on a Zoom call, which was also quite new to me, to hear about the public pre-K option for my oldest. The principal of the local elementary school started with an overview of the curriculum, goals for the year, etc., but it was what she said next that really struck a chord with me. You know when you get really good advice and you think to yourself, *I know I'm going to need to remember this some day?*

Well, while sitting on my bed on one of my first Zoom calls, clearly a rookie as I was unsure how to turn off my video option at this point, I heard it. Principal Bugg described the evaluation system they use to track progress of pre-kindergarteners. She said, "We evaluate using a scale of one to five. Every parent thinks they want their child to get all fives, but that is not really what you are aiming for. Your goal should be a well-rounded kid consistently aiming for fours." A four means they have mastered the concept but left room for fun. There is nothing wrong with a five, but a standard of perfection will only breed heartbreak. She went on to describe how, in our society today, we are so focused on our kids being "better than" that we forget about our kids doing their best, and often when we push for perfection across the board, it comes at a steep price.

My mind was spinning like the rainbow wheel of my Mac. I think this was the state in which it remained stuck for all of 2020—married to an emergency medicine physician and feeling very helpless during the scariest time of my life. Every decision felt really weighty, but especially parenting choices. Was I going to screw up my kids permanently during the pandemic? Had I already done so?

One of the hardest parts about that time was comparing my choices to other people's decision-making. Not only were we drowning in decision fatigue of our own, but now we were facing rampant judgement, which was familiar to me from the tell-tale mommy wars I'd known since I started showing my first pregnancy bump.

Our generation of parents both loathe and admire the participation trophy. It's fine for the other kids, but not our precious angels. Our kids are clearly superior to the other children because if they aren't special, then what does that say about us?

Nothing knocks you off your maternal high horse quite like having a kid who does something aggressive toward another kid. Both of mine had biting phases, and when my second was born, my oldest had a hitting phase. The hot, cheek-burning feeling of watching your child, whom you know to be good-natured, hurt another is devastating. This is especially true when you attribute their perfectly normal developmental behaviors to your own failure.

"Not *my* child. *My* child would never."

Per the American Academy of Child and Adolescent Psychology, biting typically occurs in ages one through three and is usually a response to jealousy or retaliation, but it can also be due to tooth eruption.

Hitting is another common tactic used by toddlers and preschoolers. When handling two mini aggressors, separate them first. Next, comfort the hurt child. Finally, address the aggressor. It is important to note that most children go through some phase like this. Less than pristine preschool behavior is in no way a reflection of your parenting. Turn the inward self-doubt into energy to work through the issue.

I wish I were half the mother I thought I'd be when I judged other moms when I was younger and childless. Ignorance truly is bliss. I think that is why we make those judgmental statements that get under other moms' skin like a wayward splinter.

"Sarah is walking, but I see Eli is still doing his awkward little crawl. I wouldn't worry."

"My daughter is reading. Is yours close?"

"Not sleeping through the night? Hmmm, have you tried essential oils? I'm sure you know I sell them. I've DMed you about it."

"Still nursing? Don't you feel like it's weird that he can, you know, ask for your boob?"

"Yes, yes, she's only forty-seven months and playing the violin. It's all about structure."

"Oh, I went back to work so my daughter knows that she doesn't have to grow up to only be a mom. You know, she can have dreams."

"Oh, well, we don't do screens."

"Oh, well, we don't do Santa."

"Oh, well, we don't do childhood fun—only kale and wooden toys."

It's truly exhausting. Your child is not perfect, just as you are not perfect. Motherhood can be an Olympic sport of one-upping, but it's best not even to play that kind of game.

I believe the concept of mommy wars started when women began to have the choice of whether to participate in the work force because it caused a split between working moms and stay-at-home moms. I have incredible respect for working mothers. Per most research on mental load, working mothers—even those who out work in terms of hours or income— still tend to handle the day-to-day, abstract needs of the family. These needs are known as "mental load" and include various responsibilities, such as permission slips, doctor's appointments, and birthday cards. It is not that male partners are not capable or even interested in these things, but society's rearing of women assigns us such roles.

The concept of mommy wars has moved beyond its inception with the working versus staying home binary because many women utilize a hybrid approach. Now, it has permeated other areas of mothering. Per Abetz and Moore's research, "Welcome to the Mommy Wars, Ladies," when mommy wars move to the realm of technology, they can be classified under a new term: "combative mothering."

"Combative mothering manifests discursively through the metaphor of the mommy wars, which has previously described antagonisms between working and stay-at-home mothers, but more recently has shifted to describe animus between myriad parenting philosophies and practices." Any parenting choice is up for debate—from how you feed your baby solid food or purees to baby-led weaning to whether you use cloth diapers.

Most of us have fairly idyllic expectations about what our children will be like. Although we may not like to admit it, many of us are truly looking to self-improve through our children. Maybe a mother who was a wallflower will put her daughter in seven social activities so as to not repeat the same pattern or a father who narrowly missed a college football scholarship will misguidedly force the sport on a kiddo who would rather be sketching.

Your child will never be exactly who you envision them to be. They will be better—perhaps more complex, but better. A favorite utterance of my father is, "I always prayed for healthy, intelligent children. I forgot to pray for uncomplicated." Sorry, Dad. But now, as a mother, I get it.

Word to the wise, if your child is born with something you don't expect, I don't recommend googling while you are freshly postpartum. When my son was born, I noticed a blackish purple bruise covering his left hand, arm, chest, and back. The nurse checked his oxygen saturations to make sure he was receiving adequate blood flow to the extremity and, I'm sure, to rudimentarily rule out some kind of cardiac defect. No one could definitively tell me what was going on, whether the mark was a birth injury from my three hours of pushing or a birthmark. From my own googling, my husband and I decided it was like a capillary malformation called a port wine stain birthmark.

We are fortunate that our little boy's birthmark, while extensive and requiring lifelong laser treatments under general anesthesia to keep the vasculature healthy, is not associated with other medical complications. When I first started my internet scouring, I saw a lot of scary words like "seizure disorders," "pediatric glaucoma," and "brain involvement." Admittedly, I didn't handle it all that well.

Part of me knows that every person has some sort of challenge whether it's a physical, medical, emotional, or other difference. As my stoic husband likes to remind me, "Adversity builds character." But I didn't want my sweet, innocent infant to feel any pain. I didn't want him to undergo painful procedures, face potential bullying from peers, or deal with being different.

One day I was in a clothing store trying to buy some postpartum jeans in a larger size—already a vulnerable position for a new mom, and the salesclerk, who looked to be about twelve years old, peered into the stroller and commented, "Oh, what a sweet baby. If only he didn't have that terrible rash." I threw the jeans on the counter and tersely said through tears, "It's just a birthmark"—barely holding back a four-letter word epithet.

Since that day, I have grown as a mother, especially as one of a child who has something unique about him. I am not proud of my initial feelings of *Why me? Why my baby?* I know that behind all that initial googling, there are real families and real babies facing very difficult medical complications. Of course, I know that. I spent the better part of a decade caring for medically complex children in the pediatric ICU. But it is still a challenge.

One such thing that has helped me to become a better woman and mother, though I still have acres of room to grow, is finding women who are examples of light in motherhood. I love speaking with Megan Hart Smith. Megan is a mother of two: Elijah (five years) and Abigail (twenty months). Abigail was born with cystic fibrosis that was not diagnosed until her newborn screen; that special test they do in the hospital returned after some complications with her bowels and breathing after birth earned her a NICU stay.

Megan is the mother I aspire to be. She takes the daily two-and-a-half-hour routine that managing baby Abby's CF requires in stride, making it sound all the sweeter with her Little Rock, Arkansas accent. She is the gentlest woman, but she has turned her passion for her daughter into a career in advocacy by working for the Oklahoma Family Network. "I would never really be outspoken [before]," she said. "I would share stuff, but now I feel like I have a duty. I never want Abigail to feel ashamed that she has cystic fibrosis or scared to tell somebody." Megan also went on to tell me about the fear that she has of making sure her son, who has no health issues, feels included since Abigail's care takes so much time and energy.

While most of us cannot relate exactly to what it is like to have a child with such medically complex needs, as according the Cystic Fibrosis Foundation, only thirty thousand people currently live with CF in the US, we can relate to comparing our child to others and wanting the best for them.

Whether your baby is slower to walk, has a unique birthmark, or needs breathing treatments each morning, we know that each child adds beauty to this life. Our culture of highly competitive mothering can pull us into dark places where we only see the differences or even see them as our own failures. This is despite the fact that every child, every *human*, has hurdles to overcome. Of course, it is common humanity to worry about things working out for your child, but we also know the resilience of children.

People used to ask me how I could work with critically ill pediatric patients. I would always respond with, "Kids are fighters, adults give up." And I believe that to be true. Somewhere along the way, we lose faith in our own ability to persist. We stop spinning gleefully in front of the full-length mirror. We notice our imperfections rather than our own beauty in the twirly skirt of a princess dress. We start noticing how we aren't like others. We start to compare. Here is where we should take a note from our babies and lean back into our Disney princess three-year-old-selves. We believed we were different, unique, and beautiful, and we couldn't be stopped.

CHAPTER 7

THE ROLE OF SOCIETAL PRESSURE & SOCIAL MEDIA

———

"I guess they always end up making me feel like I'm not welcome to be myself."

—CHRISTINE RICCIO, *AGAIN, BUT BETTER*

It was about 3 a.m. on one of my last shifts before I left my contract nursing job to have my son, becoming a full time stay-at-home mom—a decision my husband and I made together by weighing personal happiness, goals, and the cost of childcare. With both of us having unconventional hours working in the inpatient hospital setting, we couldn't use typical daycare. This fact combined with my occasional burnout and feeling as if I was in a holding pattern made the decision for us. While I loved the patients and families of the pediatric intensive care unit, I was starting to internalize their pain more as I got closer and closer to becoming a mother myself. I didn't think I was ready for graduate school, though I toyed with the idea.

I sat watching the EKG tracings and other vital signs of my two ICU patients bounce along as I shoved some leftover stir-fry into my mouth for my middle-of-the-night "lunch break." One of my good friends and colleagues perched on the desk with her bowl of Caesar salad and asked point blank, "So when you quit, what are you going to do all day?" Still mid-chew, I thought, *Well, I think I'll take care of my baby.*

She quickly followed up with, "Just don't be one of those stay-at-home moms who parks on the couch while her children run wild all day. And aren't you going to feel bad not contributing to your family?" I sat in stunned silence, which is rare for me. I often wish I could will myself to be silent as I hear a snarky retort exiting my lips. And this, my friends, was my very first experience with the working mom versus stay-at-home-mom drama, but it was certainly not the last.

I did think that staying home would be easier than it is. The hardest part to me is the monotony. This isn't a pity party. I could go back to work, shift some things around, and make it happen. But I think if you interview 100 percent of moms, no matter their breakdown of childrearing to working inside/outside the home, 101 percent of them will say this crap is hard.

I won't pretend there is one way to combine work and mothering. There is only your way and what works for your family. I have friends who have to work and friends who need to work. I have friends that thrive at staying home, making crafts from sunup to sundown. I am somewhere in between. I choose to stay at home because the cost of not doing so didn't make sense and because I felt ready to leave my career at that point. That does not make me lazy, though I will acknowledge the privilege I have that affords me that flexibility.

So much of our restlessness can be boiled down to unmet expectations—this lofty idea that we will be completed as women when we give birth. We believe we'll be perfect mothers with chocolate chip cookies and tidy homes. Our kids will *never* behave like *that*. Maybe on some level we know motherhood will have challenges, but many of us don't expect the changes that really occur. These expectations of perfection, strengthened by social media and societal expectations, translate into disappointment, and—as Brené Brown says—often into resentment.

The universal uniting factor of motherhood seems to be guilt: guilt for not contributing financially if you make the choice to stay home and guilt for missing out on milestones if you maintain your pre-baby career. Did you just use a disposable diaper instead of cloth? *Guilt.* Did you bottle feed instead of breastfeeding? *Guilt.* Did you fail to make a handprint craft for each grandparent for every bank holiday this year? *Guilt.* Want to make yourself feel nice and guilty? Just find your ideal stereotype of a mom on social media.

It's 10 p.m. and instead of sleeping, which is what normal people do when they are tired, I am scrolling though Instagram. I compare my life and my "following" to that of people who have it so much more together than I do. It's a bad habit that I tell myself I will quit but can't seem to break, like secretly liking Miley Cyrus or putting my fancy knives in the dishwasher. Motherhood is raw and unfiltered. Social media portrays the exact opposite of that, a curated snapshot that may be utter falsehood. It's terrible that the point is to get people to follow you without actually making genuine connection. Furthermore, if you dive into the motherhood accounts with the greatest number of followers, you'll find they all present scenes I can barely find in my own life: blissful kids in a three-tone color scheme. But we buy into it.

Why? Just watch the instant hit *The Social Dilemma,* the smash Netflix documentary on how social media permeates our psyche and exploits our insecurities, such as our needs for approval and connection, in brilliantly subtle ways. These two needs become especially tender during early motherhood. Being up in the middle of the night to feed a baby can feel like you are the only person in the world awake. I used to chew on ice and compulsively purchase home organization items off Amazon while watching reruns of *Parks and Rec* to stay awake. Connect on social media, and you'll see a community of mothers making you feel less alone.

Chrissy Teigan pivoted from model to household name with her social media presence. Chrissy, a mother of two and advocate of honesty in motherhood on social media, is married to famed singer John Legend. While the majority of us may not be able to relate to being on the cover of a magazine, most of us can relate to her social media feed. "When Luna [her daughter] is awake, I want her to sleep and when she is asleep, I want her awake," Chrissy said. "This is my parenting life."

Oh, we've all stared at the clock at the stroke of 4 p.m., praying that bedtime would come galloping in like a knight on horseback only to sneak into our babes' rooms to watch their eyelashes rest on their freckle-sprayed cheeks. They are just delicious when they sleep. Chrissy is a model of how social media can connect us—proving even celebrities are not immune to the impact of errant toddlers, sleepless nights, or postpartum pain. Conversely, some of her feed reads like a cautionary tale for stranger judgement. For example, Teigan and Legend recently shined a much-needed light on the tragedy that is pregnancy loss with the miscarriage of their third child, a decision for which she received a lot of judgement.

Recently, some of Teigan's earliest tweets on the social media platform Twitter have gained national media attention for cyberbullying. I'd be remiss if I didn't mention this, though I don't want to pile onto her story; the actress has apologized on social media and via an article on the platform Medium, though the pain inflicted on the victims cannot be backspaced. I instead share this information to shed light on the powerful impact of our words. Of course, we can hurt a friend by something we say in person, but never before in our society has the ability to pass judgement on a total stranger without context run so rampant.

Teigan shares in her apology, "In reality, I was insecure, immature and in a world where I thought I needed to impress strangers to be accepted. If there was a pop culture pile-on, I took to Twitter to try to gain attention and show off what I at the time believed was a crude, clever, harmless quip. I thought it made me cool and relatable if I poked fun at celebrities."

Whether we like it or not, social media has infiltrated our world. According to Brenda and Baker's study, while most new moms still rate their partners as their main source of support when problems arise,

- 99 percent turn to the internet to answer parenting questions,

- 89 percent use social media sites for parenting/pregnancy advice,

- and 84 percent consider social media friends a form of social support.

Is that bad, or is that good? I think it's both. If we can shield ourselves from expectations of "completeness" or "perfection," which will inevitably lead to disappointment, then the connection can be a great thing. But for every silly meme you read that makes you feel seen as a mother, there's a woman who gave birth six minutes ago with perfect hair extensions and a six pack.

In looking at real women, where does the pressure to have it all come from? Is it intrinsic, or is it thrust upon us by society and perpetuated by social media's stylized versions of our roles? I think a lot of it comes from things we've internalized—words that were not intended to be sharp but have left lasting wounds, often spoken by other women:

"Does it bother you to be wasting that college degree at home with babies?"

"Does your baby ever call the nanny 'Mommy' since she spends more time with her than you?"

"I am so glad you stay at home. After all, that is what women who can't hack it in their careers are meant to do."

Maybe we should just come out and say that we are all drowning a bit and finding someone that looks like they are more tired of treading water than ourselves makes for a pretty good scapegoat.

Add on top of that the pressure to maintain a lovely but not too grand house that you clean yourself to spotless perfection, a husband who wants you in bed all the time, but on your terms, and 2.3 children who eat sushi, play the violin, hate screen time, and smell constantly of the coconut oil you hand-made to make their skin soft.

Or maybe you don't have to do all of that, but at least do some of it better than that other woman.

In order to better capture what this pressure looks like for real women, I spoke with some friends in different life circumstances than my own.

One such a friend, a pediatrician, said one of the questions she gets asked the most is, "How can you leave your babies at home to care for other people's?" My cheeks turned pink even reading this response from her because 1) who would have the audacity to say something like that to someone in such a serving career path? and 2) this is a judgement I am wholly shielded from as a stay-at-home mom.

Another mom I spoke with built her business from the ground up, winning multiple awards in her field. Upon announcing her pregnancy with her third child, she was met with mixed feelings from family members. Some said things like, "Why have more when you are already stretched so thin and needing day care?" Cool. I don't remember her asking you for money, to babysit, or for your nose in her business.

And finally, a third mother was asked by a family member if she regrets "wasting money" on a college degree since all she does now is "babysit" her own kids all day. Babysitting? I must be doing this stay-at-home mom thing all wrong then. If this is babysitting, I get to leave at 10 p.m. and get at least ten dollars an hour. (Calm down, Nancy. It's a joke.)

Why for the love of all things holy do we speak to other women this way? Why do we leave negative comments on their posts? The way we like to fancy ourselves keyboard gangsters in the motherhood judgement department is its own additional topic. I think we often want to blame toxic masculinity or the patriarchy for our struggles, and although those forces are of course problems, we often stab ourselves in the foot! How a woman chooses to raise her babies, how many of them to have, how to care for them, and similar choices are none of your damn business.

Are we ever going to be able to do away with the societal pressure to be both career women with it all and Susie Homemaker? Probably not. But we can take comfort in the realization that we are all in this together. In *I Thought It Was Just Me (but it isn't)*, Brené Brown—or America's therapist, as I like to call her—discusses how every one of us faces the same types of pressures. Even in her own TEDx Talk which followed up her first, she asserts that she wasn't going to go down the rabbit hole of reading the comments, but after doing so devolved into peanut butter and *Downton Abbey*. If even Brown handles pressure with *Masterpiece Theatre* and treats for some time before picking herself back up, there is grace in the common humanity of this experience. Mama, you are not alone even if you feel the pressure. But good news is, as we will discover later in section three, there are things we can do about it.

CHAPTER 8

THE ROLE OF "THE PERFECT MOTHER"

"Find the perfection in every moment instead of trying to make every moment perfect."

—DONNALYNN CIVELLO

6:22 a.m. The text message arrives: "No school today due to inclement weather."

Okay, I think. *Put on your happy face. I know you don't like change. You don't like things not going according to plan, but we are going to have the perfect snow day. What does the perfect snow day mean? It means we're going to have pancakes. We are going to do crafts. We're going to play, and I won't think about the laundry piling up or the fact that they are mixing Play-Doh colors. It's going to be all* perfect *and look like a damn Instagram photo—*"perfect" being the operative word.

Get up, make coffee, and greet already feral children. They start whining at approximately

6:43 a.m. to go out and play in the snow. Unfortunately, it's 19°F outside. Although letting the kids play in the snow would allow me to finish my coffee while it's still somewhat warm, it's probably not the best parenting decision. I take a deep breath and remind myself that the *perfect* snow day doesn't involve a snarky mother. I pour cereal. *No, what am I thinking? Not cereal! That isn't special.* I'll search for a super complex recipe to make cinnamon roll pancakes from scratch, because *perfect* snow days involve pancakes, not cereal. *Get it together!*

7:30 a.m. While eating the pancakes that look nothing like the picture and taste like the discarded cereal box, I listen to a diatribe from the toddler on how Daddy makes better pancakes than Mommy because, well, he does. I blindly scroll through social media to see all the other smiling mothers on their *perfect* snow day. They have already made gingerbread houses using the kits they ordered from Amazon four days ago because they were smart enough to watch the weather and know that a snow day was coming. I awoke surprised, therefore unprepared.

It's okay. I once made a Roman bath out of sugar cubes for my Greek mythology project in middle school. I've got this. I look up how to make gingerbread while scouring the pantry.

10:10 a.m. I then Google how to make gingerbread without molasses. I convince two kids that it would be so much fun to make a gingerbread house (without molasses). I put everybody in matching aprons, snap a photo, and try to hold my breath because someone just fell off a chair and somebody else put her finger in her nose before sticking it into the dough.

I am now a level four gingerbread architect trying to hand cut pieces for my Frank Lloyd Wright-inspired gingerbread house. I'm invested.

11:45 a.m. Now dripping sweat, I send the minis outside in the snow. Getting kids in snow gear is a HIIT workout. Next, I attempt to make glue out of sugar and melt caramel into a pan to build my architectural masterpiece. Said house ends up looking like a gingerbread Unabomber shack. I am flour-smeared, holding back tears for the perfect snow day that has been anything but perfect.

1:34 p.m. I pull out all the Halloween candy I can find stuck in the recesses of the freezer and start sticking it on with icing that I made from my forty-seventh attempt at making icing.

2:03 p.m. Someone is now going to vomit from Halloween candy overindulgence. It's a lesson we have all learned and also a lesson I am not prepared to lead like Robin Williams in *Dead Poets Society* on this snow day.

2:47 p.m. The gingerbread house starts to come together. Kids are laughing. I take a deep breath for the millionth time today.

5:30 p.m. Remember that skittles with a Tums chaser aren't actually dinner. Kids' choice—that's what we should do; that makes a *perfect* snow day. We'll call it appetizer night, which basically means anything that's already in the fridge that can be cut into small pieces and thrown on a plastic plate at the counter.

6:45 p.m. Mama is tired from trying to make a *perfect* day that has felt anything but *perfect*. Bathe the grubby kids who are covered in melted snow, sweat, candy, gingerbread, and that stickiness that kids always seem to get when they've been playing at home all day.

7:30 p.m. I tuck the minis into bed a little bit early because they've exhausted themselves playing in the frigid weather, eating too much sugar, and fighting all day long. I tuck them in, and the oldest says to me, "Mom, this was a perfect day."

From Carol Brady's shag to June Cleaver's apron, women have been trying to reach unattainable perfection for generations, yet we ask why we, as women, judge ourselves so harshly. What is it about this version of who we think we should be that we're not living up to that seems to permeate every angle of our lives?

It has, in fact, permeated every angle of our lives. From the dolls we played with as little girls to the media we watched, we have been in training to be perfect mothers from the beginning, but that's impossible.

As in the story above, we spend so much time worried about the next thing that we miss the moments happening now. But our kids see them. That's the beauty of childhood. They stop and pick dandelions to blow and make wishes when all our adult brain sees is, *Geez, I need to weed the garden.*

I didn't understand what being a perfectionist actually is for a long time. I formerly believed perfectionists to be the fluffed and manicured women who always seemed to be working out, baking, and running a company on seven minutes of sleep. But perfectionism is setting an impossible standard for yourself only to be disappointed or distressed when you don't achieve superhuman status.

I have always wanted to be a mother, so naturally (or so I naively thought) I was going to be excellent at it. I read the books and did the Googling only to discover a lot of these "styles" of parenting seemed really unnatural to me. On a trip to visit family before my son was born, my aunt gave me the best piece of mothering advice I have received to date: "Parent within your own personality." If you are laid back and chill, super strict routines and rules will make you uncomfortable and inauthentic.

One morning, I was doing a stellar job, and I actually don't mean that sarcastically. My husband was working the weekend at the hospital, and I had it together. Laundry was going, actual breakfast was made, and the kids were clean-ish. I was just about to lay infant Avery down for her nap when I heard a click from outside her door. Panic struck the core of my soul. In what I thought previously was a stroke of mom genius, I'd placed a child lock on the outside of her door so her big brother couldn't go in and wake her from her nap, as had been his new habit; however, I was now locked with her in her room. My son, who had freshly turned two years old, was wandering the rest of the house solo. Ten minutes of pleading and whining with him later, I climbed, braless and in my pajamas, out the first floor window and into our backyard. Never pat yourself on your proverbial parenting back too early.

Andrea Jansen, a Swedish mother, puts the struggle perfectly in her TEDx Talk, "The Perfect Mother Does Not Exist." Jansen describes herself younger and childless having dinner with her parents and explaining how, when she is older, she will figure out how to "have it all." She goes on to say that maybe some people can't have it all, but she can "be an exception." In response to Andrea's declaration, her mother is very quiet—as if to say, "We'll see."

Jansen jumps forward to her life as a working mother in Sweden, where—she jokes—you can't even pack bananas for preschool because the government says they have "too much sugar." We would be in some serious trouble here in the United States without our calorie-laden kids snacks. She states this to exemplify the intangible pressures that seem to close in on mothers from all sides. It's the famous, "Work like you don't have children, and mother like you don't work." conundrum. We must be healthy, be slim, and work out, but cook gourmet meals from scratch. We must be sexually appealing to our partners, but remember to not be too sexualized, as we are mothers now. We have to stay late at work, but never be late to pick up our kids from daycare. Stay home and have a gorgeous, farm-inspired, brand new house that never gets dirty even though we have kids. Be patient and never yell but set age-appropriate limits. Never get sick or sleep but make time for "self-care." Be everything all the time without complaining. Easy, right?

We need to redefine what it means to "have it all." What does that mean for you? Having it all means you are going to have to change your standards or outsource something—maybe a lot of somethings. Are you going to outsource the daytime care of your children so that you can have a fulfilling career, and that's how you have it all? Are you going to stay home with your kids, and be the main care provider for them while leaning on your partner financially, and that's how you have it all? Maybe we need to take a step back and, instead of looking to "have it all," look to all we have.

What is it about us as women that makes the word "outsourcing" sound so much better than "asking for help?" To me, outsourcing sounds like I am still in control, albeit of a three-ring circus, whereas asking for help feels like an admission of failure.

We must stop trying to define success in motherhood with a one size fits all lens. I saw a meme on social media about being the Pinterest mom or being the party-planning mom and how we try and be all these different definitions of mothers at the same time. When, really, your God-given gift might be *one* of these types, or maybe you're meant to break the mold and become your own type altogether. We were never meant to be the perfect housekeeper, the perfect stay-at-home mother, the perfect full-time working mother, the perfect nurse, doctor, firefighter, and chimney sweep all at the same time.

No one can do that.

In a 1991 commencement address at Georgia Tech, Brian Dyson shared a beautiful metaphor about keeping all the balls in the air. He argues that some balls are glass, and some are rubber:

Imagine life as a game in which you are juggling some five balls in the air. You name them—work, family, health, friends, and spirit—and you're keeping all of these in the air. You will soon understand that work is a rubber ball. If you drop it, it will bounce back. But the other four balls—family, health, friends, and spirit—are made of glass. If you drop one of these, they will be irrevocably scuffed, marked, nicked, damaged, or even shattered. They will never be the same. You must understand that and strive for balance in your life.

I think most of us have more than five balls. Certainly, you have more than one rubber ball. The rubber balls represent things of lower priority, while the glass balls tie to your core, your character, your soul. Your goal while juggling balls isn't to keep them all in the air because that's impossible. Everyone, and I mean *everyone*, will occasionally drop a ball or five. The goal is to only drop those that will bounce back. Never let a glass ball shatter. Never drop a piece of your soul. Sometimes you may have to hand your glass balls to a friend or get some help carrying them. After all, the perfect mother does not exist.

CHAPTER 9

THE ROLE OF BODY IMAGE AND MATRESCENCE

"Understanding the difference between healthy striving and perfectionism is critical to laying down the shield and picking up your life. Research shows that perfectionism hampers success. In fact, it's often the path to depression, anxiety, addiction, and life paralysis."

—**BRENÉ BROWN,** *THE GIFTS OF IMPERFECTION*

When I was a teenager, I had a pretty severe eating disorder—severe enough to land me in inpatient treatment during my senior year of high school. My team of providers recommended against reading material that could be considered triggering. So of course, I bought a book called *Wasted* by Marya Hornbacher and read it cover to cover. Nothing is quite like the forbidden fruit.

Hornbacher is one the few women whose anorexia pushed her down to a weight of barely fifty pounds while still surviving.

Most of our experiences aren't so severe, but when your view of the perfect body is so distorted, hearing a story about someone who flirted so closely with death and lived can serve as justification: "See, *I'm* fine."

This detrimental, unattainable goal setting isn't unique to disordered eating; I also see it mirrored in motherhood. We strive for an unattainable goal of perfection both in action and in physical being so much that we move into the domain of self-harm rather than self-improvement.

There is a cultural distaste for the postpartum body that exists in the realm of "bouncing back." This even stretches to feeding shame for nursing mothers. I know that there are some beautiful positive body positivity campaigns out there now, but they still pale in comparison to the countless racks of grocery store magazines highlighting

"How Princess Kate Got Her Abs Back,"

"Don't Settle for a Mom Bod,"

"Shed Your Winter Weight,"

or my personal pet peeve: "Bounce Back After Baby."

If it took nine months for our bodies to change, it should take at least that long for them to revert. Because your bones and organs literally shift during pregnancy, they may never be what they were before, and that is okay. Your worth isn't measured in the number on a scale or a denim label.

I know this may not be a popular stance, but there are companies that directly prey on the societally driven insecurities of freshly postpartum women. At this point, many of us need to be reminded to shower, not inundated with poorly veiled messages from "experts"—with no degrees in health or nutrition, mind you—on how to "get your body back."

Naturally, many direct sales companies have good reputations and missions—I was even part of one—but it grinds my gears when companies earn money by using tender points to shame new mothers. I wasn't actually aware my body "went" anywhere. Sure, it changed, and I may struggle with that, but playing upon that insecurity to make a buck seems criminal.

By buying into these companies' advertisements, we become complicit in stealing joy from the core of our own experiences of motherhood. I remember distinctly looking at blogs and thinking, When *does my body go back to its twenty-year-old self?* What was wrong here—despite nursing on demand, which was the right thing to do according to some and totally wrong according to others—was that my body refused to go back to its original size. I completely ignored the science of it all. Again, that whole organs-and-bones-moving thing.

There must be space in the same way that your body makes space for the physical baby—placenta, amniotic fluid, all of that. Your heart reflects this change too because this being carves out a space that you can't fill with other things.

We have a choice. We can fight the new space created, or we can use it to redefine ourselves. We can fill the space with binge-watching Netflix and pouring one too many glasses of wine, or we can harness it.

In *Living Full: Winning My Battle with Eating Disorders*, mental health advocate Danielle Sherman-Lazar, who is the mom of three daughters, shares her journey. Danielle's eating disorder began at the tender age of nine, when she experienced extreme separation anxiety at sleep-away camp. The disorder gained a life of its own in her teen years, and Danielle battled for her life as she overcame it. In speaking with her, I found that she is incredibly open about how her struggles impact her parenting now that she has young children. She is very cognizant "to ensure that no one ever comments on [her children's] bodies or appearance but rather on their merit as individuals." She and I compared stories of our own experiences with disordered eating.

Both of us struggled immensely during our teenage years, which are commonly a time of uncertainty. Where I felt that the changes that happened to my body post-partum were difficult, Danielle found a new respect for her own body; however, she did share that she was wary of signs of relapse in periods of immense stress, such as when her second daughter required a NICU stay.

In her second book, Marya Hornbecher talks about her experience with bipolar disorder, and it is not uncommon to have to mental health issues that compound. My underlying diagnosis was, and most likely always will be, anxiety. Anxiety is especially sneaky during times of transition. It's an invisible force that likes to creep in like an evening shadow and grab hold of us—some more than others.

Facing adolescence is such a pull with one foot in adulthood and one in childhood, leaving no clear self-definition. Adolescence is hallmarked by changes hormonally as well as shifting of role definition from child to adult in adolescence and of independent woman to a mother with a dependent foil one another. Because the frontal lobe of the brain—our decision-making center—isn't fully developed until age twenty-five or so, impulsivity and reckless choices, which are quintessential stereotypes of teen life, actually do have a scientific basis. Without having the experiences of adulthood, teens cannot always think through rationally what adult consequences lie on the other side of a decision. Experience is the wisest teacher.

If we look to developmental research, Abraham Maslow's work stands out as key. Many of us may have heard of the hierarchy of needs, which basically means one cannot move to self-actualization—or realizing your full potential—if your basic needs are not met. In researching Maslow, who coincidentally died of a fatal heart attack jogging in place poolside per doctors' instructions due to a heart condition (what a way to go), wasn't so much about a pyramid approach, but more about looking at a set of needs required to be our best selves. In a 2018 *Scientific American* article, Scott Kaufman highlights some of these needs. If we look at them in the context of what is often missing during the transition to motherhood, we can see where we need to start.

Here's an abbreviated list of some principles Kauffman puts together based on Maslow's needs as well as my commentary on what I find to be present or generally missing in the early phases of parenting. There is much more research where this came from, but I know not everyone gets an uninterrupted night's sleep and has the bandwidth to dive into psychology research on the daily. These are the needs I found most relevant to new motherhood.

Maslow: Acceptance

Kaufman: I accept all of my quirks and desires without shame or apology.

Me: My body and whole life is different at this time. Acceptance is difficult.

Maslow: Authenticity

Kaufman: I can maintain my dignity and integrity even in environments and situations that are undignified.

Me: In the world of filtered social media and perfect mothers, I find it hard to show that I am struggling with juggling my new role.

Maslow: Purpose

Kaufman: I feel a great responsibility and duty to accomplish a particular mission in life.

Me: I will fiercely protect this baby with all that I have.

Maslow: Efficient Perception of Reality

Kaufman: I am always trying to get at the real truth about people and nature.

Me: I am really too flipping tired to know what is real and what isn't sometimes.

Maslow: Peak Experiences

Kaufman: I often have experiences in which I feel new horizons and possibilities opening up for myself and others.

Me: Every day is both a new horizon and the movie *Groundhog Day* with kids.

Maslow: Good Moral Intuition

Kaufman: I can tell 'deep down' right away when I've done something wrong.

Me: #Momgut is real, for sure.

Maslow: Creative Spirit

Kaufman: I have a generally creative spirit that touches everything I do.

Me: I really need to find a passion outside of organizing burp cloths to old *Friends* episodes.

If you are anything like me and have lofty, unrealistic ideas about your needs postpartum, the idea of a stranger coming in to help you sounds, at best, slightly uncomfortable and, at worst, like you aren't good enough to take care of your own baby. It's easy to forget that for generations women lived together in groups rather than in single-family homes. The support they received from the multi-generational women of their community makes our, in my opinion, super awesome meal trains look a bit pathetic. Why do we as women think that it is failure to ask for help? It's partly our own damn stubborn natures and partly the lie we tell ourselves: that ultra-independence is a strength to be prized above all others.

If we need help, are we somehow crappy feminists? I believe this mismatch between accepting support and our own naïve definitions of perceived needs after baby accounts for today's staggering statistics of postpartum mental health issues.

ON MATRESCENCE

New mothers often feel paralyzed by the sheer number of decisions and the weight of new responsibility their new little life brings. Here, experience is a difficult teacher. This phenomenon of comparing the transition to motherhood with the transition to adulthood that occurs in adolescence is called "matrescence."

Matrescence was a term with which I was unfamiliar until I stumbled upon Dr. Alexandra Sacks and her TEDx Talk: "A New Way to Think About the Transition to Motherhood." Sacks, a pioneer of women's reproductive and mental health in the field of psychiatry at Columbia, had conversations with clients which sound all too familiar: "If I wanted to be a mother so badly, why don't I feel complete or like I am good at it?" Her research referenced a long-forgotten essay by twentieth century medical anthropologist, Dana Raphael. Raphael, who coined the term 'doula' and was a huge advocate of postpartum supportive care for mothers, initially discussed matrescence as a tender time in which women need supportive care.

Alexandra Sacks, MD is a psychiatrist specializing in women, particularly those in the postpartum phase. Through her research, she noticed a pattern. Women are often disappointed in the transition that happens with new motherhood. Many come to her attempting to discern if what they are feeling is a diagnosable disorder, such as postpartum depression or postpartum anxiety. While these disorders do occur and can be very serious, often what she observes is the process called matrescence.

In her TEDx Talk, Sacks uses her own findings with some historical data to assert that not every woman dissatisfied with new motherhood has a diagnosis. In fact, if we were to normalize the experience of matrescence, a term that many think of as "the fourth trimester," or the twelve weeks following birth, our expectations will more likely match our reality, curbing some of the ever-present self-doubt and self-judgement which new mothers experience.

Sacks explains that women are also pulled in directions outside of the baby, and that is the struggle of matrescence. She states,

"If women understood the natural progression of matrescence, if they knew that most people found it hard to live inside this push and pull, if they knew that under these circumstances, ambivalence was normal and nothing to be ashamed of, they would feel less alone, they would feel less stigmatized, and I think it would even reduce rates of postpartum depression."

Matrescence is similar to adolescence, Sacks argues. "Both are times when body morphing and hormone shifting lead to an upheaval in how a person feels emotionally and how they fit into the world. And like adolescence, matrescence is not a disease, but since it's not in the familiar medical vocabulary, it's being confused with a serious condition that deserves its own expanded outreach, research, and advocacy—called Postpartum Depression."

Sacks is certainly not attempting to take away from the severity of postpartum mood disorders, which can be devastating, but to shine a light on the fact that most women do feel growing pains as they transition from childless women into mothers.

WHEN IT IS MORE THAN MATRESCENCE

The development of postpartum depression occurs in 10 to 20 percent of new mothers in the United States, according to PostpartumDepression.org. The statistics for other mood disorders such as postpartum anxiety, OCD, and PTSD are even higher, as we will discover in a future chapter; unfortunately, these conditions are not as well known. If left untreated, these disorders can wreak havoc on family life and a woman's sense of self. They can lead to suicidal ideation and completion. Treatment is available, and the diagnosis is much more readily recognized and understood today than in past generations. Typically, speaking with your OB-GYN is a good place to begin; however, if you are not getting the information and support you need, it is vital that you seek a second opinion.

CHAPTER 10

THE ROLE OF MATERNAL MENTAL HEALTH

I finally had a healthy beautiful baby girl, and I couldn't look at her. I couldn't hold her, and I couldn't sing to her, and I couldn't smile at her...All I wanted to do was disappear and die. [...] If I had been diagnosed with any other disease, I would have run to get help. I would have worn it like a badge...I didn't at first—but finally I did fight. I survived."

—BROOKE SHIELDS ON POSTPARTUM
DEPRESSION IN PEOPLE MAGAZINE

What if my husband crashes his car on the way home from work today and I am left alone with two kids?

What if something is wrong with the baby?

Anxiety was something I understood. After all, it had been my constant companion since my vague stomach aches before math tests in grade school, but this was new—these dramatic thoughts that felt like waking nightmares piercing through my day. I would later learn to call these "intrusive thoughts."

Sitting on the faux leather examination table of my OB-GYN's office, I described to her how I wasn't sleeping. I was itchy all the time. My labs were slightly off but not indicative of anything medically concerning at this point, so she asked if I'd like some medication to help me sleep and if I'd like to see a therapist. I balked, then insisted, "I am fine." But I wasn't.

Getting four hours of sleep a night due to the constant itching made my aggressive anxiety all the worse. Upon starting therapy, I learned about a condition called perinatal anxiety. Sure, I'd heard of postpartum depression and even its newer, trendier sister, postpartum anxiety—but you could get this while still pregnant? That was news to me.

I managed the itching with medication and more lab work. Thankfully, the itching didn't develop into a severe condition called idiopathic cholestasis of pregnancy, which can be very complicated and involve an early C-section. The anxiety, it seemed, had set up camp.

One of the most widely misunderstood things about maternal mental health is how it manifests. Even while experiencing perinatal anxiety that later turned into postpartum anxiety, I don't think that I fully recognized it. I didn't know until later research showed me that one of the most common manifestations of anxiety is anger. Anger is a tough emotion for women because we are shamed for expressing negative feelings and aggression. If you are an angry woman, you are a bitch. If you are an angry man, you are driven.

While I spoke to Kelly Houseman, a licensed counselor specializing in women's health and host of the podcast *Kelly's Reality*, this mama of two shared some insight on what she sees daily in her practice with women.

Anxiety can take many forms. From worrying that your baby is going to stop breathing if you're not constantly watching them or being so frazzled about a schedule— or lack thereof—that you just break down and scream or cry. I've even had a patient worried she would throw her baby off a balcony if she went anywhere with a ledge. Another less talked-about symptom is anger. Anxiety and fear can lead to angry outbursts to your partner or other children. Lack of sleep can make you say and do things that you would normally never do.

She goes on to discuss how struggling with postpartum (or perinatal) mood disorders is common and not at all a reflection on how much you love your baby or the type of mother you will ultimately be. While I constantly doubt whether I am living into being the best mother I can be for my kids, I see a plethora of examples of moms living into their truths of battling mental health while still being amazing mothers. One such example is my friend, Kristen McKinney Gardiner.

Kristen is the owner of *Driving Mom Crazy,* a blog she originally created as an outlet, but also to feature her experience as a car seat safety tech. Kristen has used her platform as a sounding board to break down the stigmas surrounding mental health—particularly stigmas related to depression, perinatal depression, and suicidality. Her raw and honest content serves as a beacon on an otherwise cropped and perfected social media scene where we often *say* we want "real," but tend to follow and like glamour and perfection.

I first met Kristen when we were both staff writers for the Oklahoma City Moms Blog Network back in 2017. Her posts were often inspiring and honest, and I was a rookie writer who barely knew how to use Gmail, let alone publish a post. She was kind enough to share her journey with me. Something she shared that really resonated with me was the guilt wave that comes after blowing up over something seemingly insignificant to your family because anxiety or depression is ramping up. Kristen said,

> "I feel a lot of guilt because I always have this vision of what parenting would be like. I just had no idea I would have these struggles—like no clue. Of course, parenting in general is always a lot harder than you think it will be. Seeing yourself unravel is a really a terrifying feeling. You don't want your kids to be affected by your condition, but you know they are, even if you're doing the best you can. Everyone says just be easy on yourself. You're doing the best you can.

I can easily relate to such moments: trying to cook dinner while answering a million questions about the eating patterns of hammerhead sharks, trying to drive in the rain while breaking up a fight about Transformers versus Elsa, trying to put a baby down for a nap when a toddler slams a door, trying to pee alone—ever.

Kristen shared with me that she started experiencing depression with her first pregnancy, and it grew stronger as the months passed. She started medication and has had peaks and valleys with her condition ever since. She knows it will never leave her; it's a part of who she is now.

"I focus a lot on trying to make sure that I apologize and explain things that have not gone the way I wanted them to so that hopefully they can know at least that this is something that I care about doing better. So they know it's not their fault."

And she's not alone. The statistics are staggering. According to Johns Hopkins University, as many as one in five women experience postpartum depression, with up to 85 percent experiencing "baby blues," a more typical mood shift during the immediate postpartum period. The most severe type of postpartum mood disorder—postpartum psychosis—affects only 0.1 percent of new mothers, unless there is an underlying history of bipolar disorder in which case the incidence is much higher—up to 30 percent. Postpartum anxiety is still more elusive to diagnose but effects an even larger percentage—up to 40 percent of new mothers per Tiffany Field's research in the *Journal of Psychiatry and Psychiatric Disorders.*

Despite increasing visibility for postpartum mental health, stigma remains; however, people like Kristen are forging new pathways for discussion. While others may not be comfortable sharing their journeys, Kristen describes speaking up as something she feels a pull to do. "Not everybody wants to do that and to share everything about their lives, but when other people do it, it lets them feel heard and seen and hopefully breaks down stigmas so that it won't be so hard for people to talk about it in the future."

Not all of us are keen to share our struggles on such an open platform, even if we are inspired by those who are able to do so. But we can still share our struggles on a more personal level with those in our everyday lives. It can be as simple as not putting on the "I'm fine" mom mask in front of our friends who have earned our trust. That second part is a big one. Vulnerability is an earned privilege of friendship.

"I'm really tired today."

"My kids are wearing me out, even though I love them."

"I'm fighting with my husband, even though I love him."

"It was hard to get up this morning."

"I worry I'm not a good mother."

"I yelled again."

"I'm feeling sad about my miscarriage."

"I think I need to call my doctor."

This kind of vulnerability, when you find people to share in it with you, can make you feel less alone. And although sharing with a friend is wonderful, it is no substitute for true treatment, like medication and therapy.

Therapy is one of the most selfless things you can do. You can stop generational patterns of behavior, explore trauma, and mend tattered relationships. But therapists are far from one size fits all. I like to think of them like hairdressers—now bear with me. I love my hair stylist. I tell her everything. And I care a lot about my hair. You all know how it feels to go to someone who just doesn't get your hair. It feels like walking in shoes that don't fit. Going to a therapist that doesn't fit you feels the same way. Don't be afraid to try out new therapists until you find the right fit.

Medication can also be a challenge if you and your health-care provider decide that is the right fit for you. It can be like getting a key to a rental car and being delivered to the airport parking lot—only you don't know which car is yours, so you start clicking the remote aimlessly, trying all of them until something unlocks. But when it does, a weight is lifted.

I was fairly resistant to the idea of medication. I have no idea why, and it's definitely not a proud practice-what-you-preach moment. Then 2020 happened. Our whole world was a giant dumpster fire, and I decided (with the help of my awesome doctor) that a little Prozac might be just the ticket. It didn't do anything at first. I just swallowed a little white pill along with my migraine medicine every night. But about six weeks in, I noticed that when my kids went through their nightly transformation into tiny terrorists post-preschool, I didn't lose my ever-loving mind. I had what I can only imagine is what other people describe as "patience." It was a slow transition—nothing Earth shattering. With the medication in conjunction with a great therapist, things that seemed difficult suddenly seemed lighter. Stay tuned for my sequel, *Dear Jesus, Send Prozac!*

You do not have to suffer under the weight of maternal mental illness, whether it be something that's been around for as long as you can remember or something that creeps in as a result of motherhood's changes. Almost every mother I know has some experience with this, and the rest of them are probably in denial. Certain factors do increase your risk, so it is a good idea to know your odds before you end up in a crisis situation:

- Family history of mental health issues
- Fertility struggles
- Underlying health issues (such as hormonal or vitamin deficiencies)
- Poor sleep
- Poor diet
- Poor social support
- Domestic abuse

I personally had very few risk factors to develop postpartum anxiety, but my biggest set up was the mismatch between my expectations and the reality of motherhood. This is a dynamic I see mirrored in many of my peers who struggle as I did. They expect motherhood to be a certain way, and when it does not go according to plan, they struggle with anxiety, then frustration, then anger, then guilt. It's a lovely cycle. Zero out of five stars. Do not recommend. Though I still often get stuck on this Ferris wheel of anxiety, particularly when I am facing something I have never done before, such as a new parenting milestone or challenge. I am getting better at recognizing the signs in myself. I can feel the tingle of anger. I don't always stop it in time, but it's a start.

CHAPTER 11

NEVER SAY NEVER

Show up late.

Show up late with coffee.

Have a kid with a crusty, runny nose.

Go out in public with *dirty* hair and yoga pants.

Go out in public with *dirty* hair and *dirty* yoga pants.

Go shopping with kids wearing pajamas.

Bribe my pajama-clad children to behave on a shopping trip.

Carry a child screaming out of a store or restaurant under my arm like a surfboard wearing a death stare.

Take my child to the pediatrician when there's nothing wrong with her.

Wait too long to take my child to the pediatrician.

Yell.

Yell a lot.

Let my kids stay up late.

Put my kids to bed before their bedtime.

Let my kids have PBJ for breakfast, lunch, and dinner.

Take a bath twice a day.

Take a bath twice a week.

Use glitter.

Do a sensory activity.

Order everything online.

Make everything from scratch.

Drink/Swear.

Bribe for vegetables.

Bribe for behavior.

Bribe for *everything*.

Bribe with screens, candy, my 401k—*anything* for five minutes of quiet.

Over-post about my children on social media.

Talk to strangers about my children.

Stay up too late making a first birthday banner that will get thrown away the next day.

Cry at milestones.

Cry because a toddler is "being mean to me."

Cry in the bathroom.

Cry in my closet.

Laugh until I pee my pants.

Put my child ahead of my marriage.

Put myself ahead of my child.

Scroll through my phone while parenting.

Wish I'd gone back to work.

Dress my kids alike.

Dress my daughter like me.

Count green veggie straws as an actual vegetable.

Go on too many date nights.

Not go on enough date nights.

Put my self-care too far down on the priority list.

Have groceries delivered.

Abandon a grocery cart due to a crying baby.

Order pizza because dinner just couldn't be cooked.

Play instead of cook.

Cook instead of play.

Ignore a tantrum.

Spank.

Say, "Yes!"

Say, "No."

Forget to listen.

Judge another mother because I am having a bad day.

Judge myself because I am having a bad day.

Drink coffee until it's time to drink wine.

Pay a small fortune for an early release of a kids' movie on a streaming app

Steal Halloween candy and then pretend I don't know what happened to it

Yell at my husband because I'm tired and I know he will forgive my yelling.

Sing (and dance) to "Baby Shark."

Know which season of *Daniel Tiger* the "Love Day" episode is in (because my kids won't watch TV)

Skip pages of bedtime stories.

Make up stories.

Lie to say the park is closed.

Belt *Frozen* at the top of my lungs.

Belt '90s rap at the top of my lungs.

Love the biggest.

SECTION THREE

WHAT TO DO TO
FIND YOUR JOY
IN THE CHAOS

CHAPTER 12

FIND JOY IN RECOGNITION OF THE STRUGGLE

"We cannot solve our problems with the same level of thinking that created them."

—*ALBERT EINSTEIN*

I am bad at playing with my kids. I love to bake with them (provided I can crack the eggs) or color or do a puzzle.

But pretend play? It's honestly a struggle for me. I always wanted to be a mother—from the early ages of playing with dolls and forcing my little sister, four years my junior, to be my "baby." I didn't want to just be good at mothering, especially because becoming a mother wasn't as straight forward as I planned. Whose journey goes exactly according to plan? I figured I should relish every moment, but instead, when I sit on the floor to play whatever imaginary game my kids invented that day, I think of the dirty dishes. The sticky counters.

Mount Laundry. And I know that I am the one who is supposed to be doing those things. I forget, or rather struggle, to be present in light of all the other tasks piling up.

Now that we have identified in the first two sections of the book the common insecurities many of us face as mothers and in the second section the reasons why, let's start looking at what to do about it.

RECOGNITION OF NEEDS

Everyone and their Schnauzer suggests self-care to moms, but what does that really mean? So often we are presented with the idea that self-care is self-indulgence in our society. Eat that brownie. Get that mani-pedi. Buy the jeans. All those things are fun. I love a good brownie—I make mine with espresso!—but that's not truly self-care.

Self-care is admitting that we need things. That is it, plain and simple. We need things like balanced foods (not crazy yo-yo diets or dangerously low BMIs), enough sleep (not mommy martyrdom), and support (again, not mommy martyrdom). For me, self-care is the recognition that I am a routine person. It is boring as hell, but I am thirty-four years old, and that's life. I am the happiest not when I indulge in two extra episodes of a serial killer drama and a heavy pour of pinot noir on the pretense of self-care. Instead, I am happiest when I listen to my audiobook, do some yoga, and go to bed at a decent time. Nor is self-care scrolling through Instagram while pining for a cleaner, bigger, better life.

RECOGNITION THAT BAD MOMENTS DON'T MAKE BAD MOMS

Part of the key to finding joy even in the parts of motherhood that are a struggle is realizing that bad moments don't make bad moms. Pretending to be perfect is exhausting, but negativity is also contagious. Either one of these extremes can put us on a path to misery.

According to the Harvard University Stress and Development lab, both the ideas of positive reframing, or putting our thoughts into a more positive light, and examining evidence, or looking at facts over feelings, can really help. "Other strategies for reappraisal include reminding yourself that thoughts aren't facts, identifying extreme language (e.g., I will always feel this way; things will never get better) and rephrasing with less extreme words, questioning the assumptions or biases that led to your interpretation, and taking on someone else's perspective (e.g., if you told someone else about the situation, would they interpret it the same way?)."

Taking a moment to breathe and recognize my thought patterns has helped me tremendously, although I often get caught in the patterns of perfectionism or overly negative thinking. Both of these reactions are normal and happen because we care deeply about the outcome of our child rearing. What I didn't know before counseling and more research is that negativity and perfectionistic thinking are actually linked. For example, if I can't do something perfectly, then why bother?

My baby doesn't sleep.

Perfectionist: *I can function without enough rest.*

Negative: *I will remind all of my childless friends to sleep now because they never will again.*

Recognition and honor: *I am exhausted, and this is hard. I should tell a friend, but it doesn't mean because sometimes I'd rather sleep than parent that I am a bad mother.*

I cannot stop the whining.

Perfectionist: *I will ignore tantrums in public and overreact in private.*

Negative: *I wouldn't have to yell if you didn't whine. I'll just pour wine until I don't really care.*

Recognition and honor: *It's making me feel anxious that I cannot control my child's negative behavior. I worry that it's a reflection of bad parenting or that my child just doesn't have a good personality. I am going to remind myself that whining is normal, but that I might need a break to be my best self.*

My kid is a picky eater.

Perfectionist: *I will make Pinterest bento boxes for every meal and snack and pretend I am not heartbroken when my kids still won't touch the cheddar rose I made.*

Negative: *Whatever, eat what you want.*

Recognition and honor: *This makes me feel like if I were a better mother they would eat. I need to remind myself pickiness is often a phase but making food a battle upsets us both.*

My baby's peers are developmentally ahead.

Perfectionist: *I will just ignore the comments—even those attempting to help—because I don't want the judgement.*

Negative: *It's probably because I didn't breastfeed/do tummy time/have a schedule.*

Recognition and honor: *Even though I know every child develops at their own pace, being behind feels like a reflection on me. It makes me feel embarrassed when someone asks why they aren't keeping up.*

Okay, so we have these thoughts, and it's hard to reframe them. What do we do instead?

Many of us numb them out.

RECOGNITION OF NUMBING BEHAVIOR

I read a post a few years back denouncing the mommy wine meme culture, and I'll admit I was offended. *Who cares if people make wine jokes?* I thought. *Get a thicker skin.* Of course, people care. Alcohol abuse is a serious mental and physical illness. Yes, raising children is hard. Why did I get offended? Probably because I had given in to the temptation to pour a glass or three of "mommy juice" at five o'clock or because I knew what it felt like to wake up with a headache after a girl's night and still have to parent. As mothers, we don't like anything that makes us feel less than amazing at parenting—especially the truth.

Drinking has never been a serious problem for me, though I'm sure that at times I've used it to numb rather than relax. I listened to a TEDx Talk called "Grey Area Drinking" by Jolene Park because a friend of mine recommended it to me. Park says, "What people didn't know was how much I loved the 'off' switch that wine provided to my 'on' and often anxious brain." *Well, if that ain't the truth,* I thought. In her talk, Park explores on a scientific level how to replace unhealthy coping mechanisms with healthier ones based on the neurotransmitters suffering. For example, if you drink to relax, you may be suffering from a lack of GABA (a neurotransmitter).

So often we hear about recognizing problems in our lives when they hit that "rock bottom" situation. I don't say that to judge the millions of women who have been in a rock bottom and climbed out of it; that is heroic beyond measure. But I say it to assert that maybe if we could recognize our issues in the grey area *and* be willing to do something about them, we may be happier, more fulfilled women.

A situation becomes a problem when we are numbing rather than coping. For example, for someone who uses alcohol without a chemical or emotional dependence, a glass of wine or two really might be a way to unwind. A bottle of wine or two is numbing—not unwinding. An episode of a silly television show is unwinding. Binging a series late into the night so that you cannot get enough rest to adequately function the next day is numbing. We as a society love to push everything good so far to the extreme that even good things become tainted. This obsession with the term self-care is a prime example. Exercise is self-care until it's an obsession that can be as unhealthy as obesity.

RECOGNITION OF *TRUE* SELF-CARE

How do we do self-care without going overboard? As mamas, we are so used to going the extra mile that our own health often becomes all or nothing. What I am learning by *a lot* of trial and error is to look for examples of healthy moderation in our lives. When researching for this chapter, I was also beginning a new workout program alongside a friend of mine. The pandemic couch potato syndrome was becoming a bit old, so I finally (begrudgingly) started the Move by Madi. Madi is a local mom in my community who has a fascinating story. After a month of her —get this—*fifteen* minute workout and her no nonsense approach to mama health, I had to learn more about her story.

I chatted with Madi—a true multitasking mom—on a Tuesday morning while she fed her youngest daughter. Madi developed her workout program for moms as something to do for herself during her husband's medical school journey. Upon sharing her simple yet effective workouts for a very reasonable membership fee, interest skyrocketed. I love Madi's attitude about her success. "It was never about making money or becoming a thing," she explained. "It was about helping women care for themselves in an approachable way."

After the birth of her second daughter, Madi suffered a brain hemorrhage while exercising in her garage. This postpartum complication could have left her disabled or left her husband a widower. As she breastfed her second daughter in the ICU, Madi was just grateful to be alive. Her story is so powerful and really harnesses what self-care should be: women supporting others to move in a positive direction. You will often hear Madi saying, "Do the workout or don't. At least just *move* your body." She's the epitome of realism, knowing you won't achieve a Kardashian bod without work, but also knows we are real people with a lot of complex needs. I am the better for knowing her.

Do I think we have to be teetotaling, balanced meal-eating, Stepford Barbies to be good mothers? Of course not. The best way to be good mothers is to *recognize* that we are humans with flaws and show that to our kids. Pretending that we are perfect and have it all together may be as damaging to our kids as being all-out messes. They need to see that we can still grow, change, and have dreams to chase.

Recognition that certain behaviors or ways of thinking may not be serving us is a wonderful foundation for growth. Many of us should try leaning into the growing pains of early motherhood because they are very normal. Even if the tenderness of growing into a new mom is normal, it can still be scary. There are things we can do to make that transition a little less overwhelming and restore some joy to this chaotic phase of shepherding little ones.

So, what do we do if we are struggling with anxiety, depression, matrescence, substance, life? That is what we will explore in this next section. Like anything in life, it is much easier said than done, but I have a few suggestions from those much smarter than myself. Find someone to talk to who won't share your stuff. And I mean that. It can be very easy to confide in some people, but not everyone is worthy of knowing your truth.

This is an excellent place for a therapist. Before you decide that you are not in "that bad of a place," pretend you are your best friend and not yourself. *Every single time* I talk to women, we're too busy for the things that are really needed, or we have to take care of someone else instead of ourselves.

I'm going to say this very clearly because, while typing this message, I probably need to hear it.

You are a person of worth.

You, regardless of what you have done, what you have said, who you have gossiped about, or what you have eaten, deserve to feel whole.

How we each get there might look different. It might look like Prozac and a therapist. It might look like yoga and church. It might look like meditation and gardening. I don't know. But actually investing in yourself to become a whole and healed person is not selfish. My pastor, a very wise man, once said in a sermon, "If you aren't dealing with your trauma, someone else is." Check and mate.

For us mamas, I'd love to believe that the motivation to better ourselves would come from within, but you and I both know it will likely come from the desire to be better mamas to our little people. Whatever it is that makes us want to be better, I think we can do it with help, finding a cohort, cultivating a relationship with a higher power—whatever that may look like for you, and finding a passion outside of being a mother.

CHAPTER 13

FIND JOY IN A COHORT OF WOMEN

"Friendship is born at that moment when one person says to another: 'What! You too? I thought I was the only one.'"

—C.S. LEWIS

Running late to preschool, again.

I used to never be late. I judged everyone who was late. I mean, how hard is it be on time? Well, now I know. My toddler inevitably had to poop at the exact time I got everyone buckled, and my nursing mom brain forgot everything until I was at the end of the driveway. *Very hard* was the answer.

Taking the route to the preschool a little faster than strictly legal via the posted signs, lest my two-year-old miss circle time and be academically disadvantaged forever, I slammed on my breaks as a rusted out pickup with more bumper stickers than sense skidded in front of me. Swerving to avoid them, I hit the curb. My dashboard aggressively lit up like Independence Day. Most aggressively, my tire pressure went twenty-eight, twenty-two, sixteen, twelve, eight, five.

Four letter words spewed from my mouth like morning sickness, which I'm sure my toddler shared for show and tell—kids, right? I managed to make it to the school parking lot before the tire got to a pressure of zero.

I called one of my mom friends in tears. She pulled into the parking lot and whisked my baby away as she headed on her errands. I waited for hours for a tow truck driver who seemed like he'd come straight from a seedy bar to tow me to the dealership. Thank goodness my friend had come to care for my daughter because I couldn't have fit her car seat with me in the cigarette-infiltrated cab of the tow truck. My husband was at the hospital, and as any married-to-medicine wife will know, he may as well have been out of town because, as the only doctor, he couldn't leave a trauma center.

My sweet friend took my daughter to the grocery store and on a few errands before taking her home to my house so she wouldn't miss her nap. I was sitting in the dealership waiting on a pricey estimate when I got a text from her.

Avery vomited, she wrote. *It's okay. I changed her and bathed her and washed her car seat. No worries. Just wanted you to know.* Hot tears stung my face as *Judge Judy* played in the lobby of the waiting room.

No other kind of friends would do this for me: only mom friends. Only friends who know how much it would suck to be stranded with a nursing baby. Only those who know how to heat up a bottle of frozen breastmilk and remember the song your baby likes so she'll eat it when she really doesn't like bottles.

Being a new mom is such a vulnerable position. Many of us have a constant marquee scrolling through our brains of *Am*

I doing this well enough? Am I screwing up my kids? What if I am wrong about everything?

It can be hard to be vulnerable with a new friend. It's all fine and good for everyone to have unique gifts and talents when they are kids, but by motherhood, you should apparently be good at everything—or at the very least be able to stay in shape, have cute kids, be sexy for your husbands, have a clean and well-decorated house, work (but not too much), and show up with homemade treats for the bake sale.

Oh, yeah, and don't forget to smile.

One of the most common things I read when I look at new mom groups on social media is comments about feelings of isolation. Fear of somehow getting this whole mom thing wrong due to matrescence, postpartum mood disorder, or simply personality can hinder us from living into our full motherhood experience, which I believe is best achieved in community with other moms.

But what do you do if you feel stuck? What if you are the only one of your friends with a baby or feel too nervous to put yourself out there with new moms?

Social media is a good place to build confidence but is not a replacement for in person connection. We all know playground mom flirting might be more awkward than bar flirting for a hook up back in the day.

"Hello, fellow mom. I see you have a tiny human who likes to throw sand. I too have one and haven't slept well since their conception. Would you like to drink the caffeine and talk about the things while trying to convince our kids they don't hate highchairs and bribing them with puffs?"

Or you can just text about how we should really do something sometime but never make actual plans.

Hey, Xander's mom. Was so great to meet you at the indoor play place. You made it so much more tolerable to be in a padded room with fifty screaming toddlers. I am sorry I can't remember your actual name, but would you like to get coffee sometime when we don't have the kids? So, in like five years?

Painful.

Finding mom friends isn't always the easiest task. We aren't living in community villages here in the United States or most of the developed world, even as we did a century ago. In fact, per a landmark study on social support in postpartum women by Negron et al., community is one of the biggest protective factors against developing postpartum depression. Women wanted this support without knowing how or being able to ask for it in many cases: "Support from partners and families was expected and many women believed this support should be provided without asking." This finding means we as women need to reach out to our friends and sisters when they may not be able to do it for themselves.

This right here is your sign from the universe to call, text, or DM that mom you planned to. After the awkward mom flirt at a playground, a lot of these relationships fizzle before we give them the chance, so swipe right—metaphorically speaking.

There are types of mom relationships with other women that are vital to cultivate as a new mom. Look for moms in the same phase of life as you and mentor moms who are more experienced than you. Same phase of life moms are people with whom you can share the sleepless nights, growth spurts, and hard and joyous moments. Even those closest to you who are not in the same phase of life may not be able to relate in the way that someone else walking the path of early motherhood could. There is just something to be said for another mother who doesn't try to offer suggestions of "back in my day" or stare at you with vacant, unknowing eyes, but instead nods along understandingly.

I had the best luck forging mom friendships when I forced myself into scheduled activities for a few reasons:

1. I could bring my child, so I didn't have the convenient "I can't get a sitter" excuse.

2. It was a scheduled thing in my calendar, so I could start packing my fifty-pound diaper bag complete with pre-dosed Tylenol, a seasonally appropriate change of clothes and vaccination record (child number one) or throw a diaper and a semi clean onesie into the trunk (kid number two) the night before.

Moms of Preschoolers is a fantastic organization that encourages mentor moms as part of its structure. In their mission statement, MOPs says, "We are passionate proponents for the value of motherhood and the influence of women." By partnering with local churches, MOPs creates communities for mothers of young children to learn from older moms to grow in spiritual depth and community. Many new moms are wary of any social organization that is so structured, but I encourage you to consider it.

Mentor moms are great for an entirely different reason. They can show you the true embodiment of the famous Gretchen Rubin quote, "The days are long, but the years are short." There is much wisdom to be gained from emulating someone who has been there and done that. I suggest finding women whom you admire and to whom you may or may not be related. I am fortunate to have a couple of these women in my life: women who have gone before me and can answer all the dumb questions I think of in the middle of the night. You know the ones—the treadmill of mom worry.

Building a network of women is something that Andrea Cottle has built into not only a passion, but also a career, running two small businesses: The Oklahoma City franchise of Fit-4Mom and her fitness wear business. I, myself, was a member of Fit4Mom for three years. Divided into different types of mom-centered fitness classes—some with and some without children present— it is designed to be a community of moms prioritizing health and wellness. Some of my very best mom friends came from this community.

Andrea is a mom of two daughters, ages four and nine months. She started with Fit4Mom as a client when her oldest was just five months old. She dragged a friend along to her first class, and she admits they were both "a bit judgmental" of the types of stay-at-home moms who would spend the day working out with their babies. But what she found was wonderful. One year later, she was an instructor and found herself "emerging from her postpartum haze." A year after that, the opportunity to purchase the franchise from the previous owner presented itself.

After growing up as primarily an only child after the death of her sister at a young age, Andrea said that finding a community of women was always important to her—from the collegiate soccer field where she served as captain to leading

Oklahoma in her over one-hundred-person team of activewear sales. Creating an environment where women support one another is her paramount goal. "As long as I am the owner, this will be a "You do you." and judgement-free zone of support," Cottle said.

Speaking of such support, Cottle recalls a time when she herself needed some extra help. Eight weeks into her second pregnancy, she found herself staring at an ultrasound screen, being given a non-optimistic prognosis which was confirmed to be a pregnancy loss ten days later. When she reached out to her Fit4Mom community support, she received love, food, and words of encouragement. She shared with me that this community, unlike many others, made her feel comfortable sharing her journey, and in those difficult moments, she somehow knew she would be okay because others had shared their experiences and walked alongside her.

Finding a cohort of women might mean stepping a bit out of your comfort zone to attend a class or go to a mom's group, but once you find your people, the juice will be worth the squeeze. Online connections are awesome—certainly great for those burning middle-of-the-night questions, but they are no replacement for real, face-to-face mom friendships. The women you meet may not end up being your best friends when you're silver haired and playing bridge, but then again, they might be. Give yourself a chance by stepping out. Remember to reach out to others because your reaching out could be what pulls them from the grips of a postpartum struggle you know nothing about.

I'd love to say I have always been the same kind of friend that mine was that day, but I haven't. Sometimes I am awesome and remember miscarriage dates and text about sick grandmas in the hospital and drop off meals for no reason, but other times, I drop the ball hard—caught up in my own mess. Not everyone in this phase is good friend material. Some of these friendships are needed but situational, and that is okay. There is a beautiful place for friendships given to us to serve one another for a season. Lean into the moment and enjoy those bidding for connection around you.

CHAPTER 14

FIND JOY IN CULTIVATING FAITH

———

"Lord, grant me the serenity to accept the things I cannot change, the courage to change the things I can, and the wisdom to know the difference."

—SERENITY PRAYER (ATTRIBUTED TO REINHOLD NIEBUHR)

I wiped the third round of tears from my eyes as I got out of the car to walk into my very first Bible study. Thirty-one weeks pregnant with my second baby, and this was the first time I ever intentionally set out to learn more about the Bible and Christianity outside of sporadic Sunday sermons since living at home with my parents. I walked into the room to find women with monogrammed cups and spiral-bound planners marking their places. Every one of them had her own personal Bible, some emblazoned with their names resting in their laps. Imposter syndrome hit me hard. *What the hell am I doing here?* I thought. *I won't fit in with these women and their trifecta of monogrammed biblical paraphernalia. Can I even say "hell" in regard to a Bible study?*

Having never been much of a wallflower, I chose a seat. The opening prayer began with a beautiful testimony to God's faithfulness. I could feel the tears pricking my eyes again. I prayed sometimes, but never aloud unless I was with the congregation of my childhood Catholic church or before a meal. Apparently, the tradition was to go around the room, introduce yourself, and say your "praise" and "prayer request." I kind of zoned out while I tried to think of something that wouldn't sound dumb in front of this group of well-dressed strangers. But when it was my turn, I admitted I was having a hard time. I'd just sent my toddler to Mother's Day Out for the first time. And then I couldn't continue. The tears fell. They were not sweet little "oh, precious pregnant girl" tears but ugly, deep tears.

The truth was I'd just acknowledged my perinatal anxiety after months of struggling with it and intrusive thoughts. One week earlier, I'd had my first appointment with a therapist, which I liked slightly more than getting a cavity filled. Self-work is, well, *work* sometimes, but it's so worth it. And these lovely souls got a front row seat to my meltdown. They showed the empathy and compassion for which I hope someday to be known.

Somehow, I went back two weeks later with barely a shred of dignity intact. Our study for that semester was Shauna Niequist's *Present Over Perfect*. She writes, "What kills a soul? Exhaustion, secret keeping, image management. And what brings a soul back from the dead? Honesty, connection, grace." While I couldn't relate to Niequist's difficulties deciding between organizing her high-powered career and family vacations (she intimidated me further as she seemed far closer to "perfect" than I would ever be), I did learn from that study that God uses women in connection with one another to teach us our worth when we struggle to find it ourselves.

So now what? How do we get out of this pattern? What do we do to lift ourselves out and reclaim motherhood for ourselves? We lean into the experience that makes us both better women and better examples for the future generations. I find some things to be vital in that journey.

I don't believe that you have to cultivate a relationship with God in a certain prescribed way to be a good mother. I do believe that the benefits of doing so are tremendous. Personally, I have always dealt with anxiety, which I am sure is fairly obvious if you've made it this far into my book. But even deeper, I struggle with self-worth, especially without the external validation of achievements or accolades.

You know what there is *not* much of in motherhood? Concrete boxes to check or people to tell you you're doing a great job at handling the invisible tasks that make the world run. How can you measure that?

If you look at how God chose to send the Savior, Jesus, to us, it's remarkable to note that he chose a mother. Not a high-powered king, chariot of fire, or Chris Angel-esque pyrotechnic, but a young mother—scared and confused just like I felt in that moment. Of course, Mary had a bit more to deal with than I did what with the whole potential stoning, immaculate conception situation. It is worth noting how many times in the Bible God comes to women in a quiet, calm, relatable way. God has a long history of meeting women exactly where they are: overwhelmed, longing for children (Sarah, Rebekah, Rachel, Hannah, and Elisabeth), drowning in struggle. While their paths look different in culture and context, many of the heartaches are timeless.

I don't think I have ever explored faith as deeply as I did when I had a child. I'm certainly not saying that those who are childless can't have that understanding. There is clearly a whole subset of people who take vows of celibacy and are immersed in religion, but for me, this was the experience.

Previously, I could not understand how a loving God could sacrifice His own child for our salvation. I could not understand what a sacrifice that was, nor the kind of love it would take to give the weary world such a gift. Even if we go back to the beginning of the Bible with Abraham and Isaac, how could you have faith strong enough to say, "I would give my child to you?" I don't think God wants to take our children up to a mountaintop for human sacrifice. I promise you I don't believe in that kind of God.

But I do believe that what he's calling us to do is to give our shortcomings over to him, to say, "I fail in this moment without the gift of divine strength." I don't have the gumption or the patience to get through this hard task of motherhood, but You do. To say, I can give this to You. You can lift me up and help me to be a better person. Help me to achieve my goals in this.

If you are someone interested in beginning a relationship with God, I can promise you these things:

- It can be hard to give up control but surrendering to the belief that you don't have to figure out your whole world alone brings an amazing sense of peace.

- Learning your worth in the eyes of God is a struggle for some of us, but it is one of the best ways to have a fulfilling life. Once you know your worth as a child of God, you will not settle for ill treatment from others who wish you harm, you will have the confidence to chase dreams you thought you didn't deserve, and you will have a place to turn when things don't work out.

- One of the most common arguments I hear for why people don't want to walk with God is that bad things happen. And to this I say, "Yes! You are right. Bad things do happen. God never promised us a life free from pain, just that we will not have to walk alone."

Jen Jewell, host of *The Messy Table* podcast, is no stranger to ministry. She and her husband have been part of Life Church, one of the largest non-denominational churches in the nation, for a long time. She's currently part of the women's ministry, where her energy, approachability, and light help women find their faith in hour-long, bite-sized nuggets. Upon listening to an episode, what you'll find is grace for yourself and grace from above. When I spoke to Jen about her podcast and its advent, she explained to me that for most of her children's early years, she was a stay-at-home mom and supported her husband's ministry. While it's a beautiful thing to be home with littles and writing, as her children grew, she found herself having a little bit more time. She prayed and prayed about what God was calling her to do. She shared one her favorite scripture passages with me:

"Without oxen a stable stay clean, but you need a strong ox for a large harvest." Proverbs 14:4 NIV

The *Messy Table* podcast was born in partnership with Life Church. She said she prayed, "God let me play." And I love that. I imagine many moms sitting on the bench in a little league game, waiting for our turn at bat. We may have made career shifts or put careers or dreams on hold to raise our little people. It is important that we don't stay on the bench too long, that we remember our gifts and our wisdom which existed before children.

Jen told me a beautiful story about a time when she felt God's presence very close to her. Her oldest son was diagnosed with febrile seizures, a childhood condition where the temperature rises too quickly, causing a seizure. At this point, her son had experienced a few, and they were prepared to watch for them when he was sick. On this particular day, he had an atypical seizure. As Jen describes, his body turned a very pale shade of white, and he went very limp and stopped breathing. She and her husband started CPR and called 911. She said she recalls very dramatically praying out to God that He would not take her son that night, and the child miraculously recovered. She was very quick to mention after this, though, that her faith is not dependent on things working out how she wants them to. I thought that this was a beautiful point because faith is not about getting our plan. Faith is about not walking alone in the journey.

As I mentioned in my story about attending Bible study for the first time, I don't think I would have considered my relationship with God to be very deep before recent years. A few things have impacted the depth of that relationship: I dealt with pregnancy loss and, for the first time in my life, admitted I was angry with God, I found a church that I enjoyed attending, and I met some other women with deep faith that radiated peace.

I consider my husband a Christian with a bit of Agnostic persuasion. When I talked to him about my newfound depth of faith, he asked, "What if you're wrong about all of this?"

"Does it matter?" I replied.

If I can feel empowered to chase my dreams and be inspired to do good for others, even if earth rather than heaven is the end of this journey, it will have been worth it.

He smiled and said, "Well, I guess you are right."

Apparently, I am not alone in these feelings. According to the Pew Research Center, the majority of American adults who follow an organized religion feel "a sense of wellbeing and spiritual peace." According to Pew, while fewer women believed in God with absolute certainty in 2014 than in 2007, dropping from 77 percent to 69 percent, American women's sense of spiritual wellbeing and peace has increased in the last decade. You don't have to be certain in your beliefs to gain a spiritual calm. God will meet you where you are.

When He does, we have to thank Him. I've had moments where I've just seen unparalleled grace come through for me. Moments when I didn't think I could get up for another night feeding. Moments when only a supernatural strength carried me through and gave me the sense that this too shall pass. Whether we are willing to acknowledge it, with help we get up the next morning and we do it again. Sure, some days aren't as good as others. Some days we do have Disney movie marathons instead of playing with our math manipulatives. Other days we thrive. We go on walks, telling stories. We laugh until we cry.

I love what the women at *Risen Motherhood* are doing to spread ministry to others in an approachable way. If you can't tell, I am a big fan of podcasts; they are great for busy moms, whether you're on work commutes or listening in the background of *Paw Patrol*. One of my favorite episodes of *Risen Motherhood* focuses on how the little years are not the lost years.

So often we see images of women rising early in the morning before kids wake to be productive, to have "me time," or maybe to do their Bible study. But in this episode, the hosts focus on how drowning in babies can make that impractical. God will find you where you are, just like He did with the woman at the well. Let yourself be filled and rest in heavenly strength so that when the challenges of motherhood arise just like a preschooler the day after Halloween—in a combination of fury and exhaustion—you will have more than your own strength to draw upon.

If you have been hurt by an organized religion or see hypocrisy, I don't blame you. I see it too. Don't let a wayward soul keep you from enjoying a faith that can be life-changing. There is a perfect community for you. I am sure of it.

If you are not interested in the idea of religion, especially in a traditionally organized sense, you can still apply many of these concepts to your life. For example, one of the strongest spiritual feelings my husband gets is watching the sunrise from a deer stand. I feel whole when looking at the ocean and "feeling the sand between my toes." Goodness, did Third Eye Blind nail it with that lyric. I get religious fulfillment in a way that might not be for you, but the beauty of community is that we can share and respect our differences.

Interested in how God promises things or "makes covenants in biblical terms? Check out this scripture passage that brings me hope: Romans 8:18.

CHAPTER 15

FIND JOY IN A PERSONAL PASSION

"The best time to plan a book is while you're doing the dishes."

—*AGATHA CHRISTIE*

Back in the spring of 2016, when I was newly pregnant with my daughter, I attended a morning class of my mommy and me fitness group. I started attending when my oldest was around four weeks old. Essentially, it's a workout program designed for moms where you put your children in strollers and exercise while entertaining the kids with Nursery Rhymes. Baby is happy, and mom gets a workout: win-win! But more than that, it's a community of moms who support one another through the journey of early motherhood.

The beginning of class always started with a question. Each member of the group would go around the circle while we stretched, warmed up, introduced ourselves and our babies, and answered the daily question. The question of the day was, "In five years what is something that you want to accomplish just for you?"

There were no restrictions, no goal too lofty. Moms began to share all sorts of interesting things. As I thought about it, I realized most of the questions every day revolved around what little Jenny's eating this week or what milestone your child has achieved that you're super excited about. These are great questions, and they're fun to talk about because I don't know a single mother who doesn't love to talk about her baby.

I, however, was almost paralyzed by the thought of answering a question that is just about what I wanted to do for *me*. Could I go back in time and be that person who was separate from my kids? As I later learned, it's not about going back in time, it's about moving forward and growing into the new person who you were meant to be.

I thought for a while. Thankfully, I was toward the end of the circle as we did our calf stretches and warmed up before our workout. I sprinkled some goldfish on my son's stroller snack tray and blurted, "I want to start a blog. And I want to be a professional writer."

I didn't know why I'd said that. I had clearly been ruminating on that thought somewhere in the recesses of my brain since it popped out so easily.

Later, the instructor who had asked the question came up to me and said, "Just do it. Start a blog." I laughed it off and didn't think about it until a couple of weeks later, when I saw an open call for contributors to the Oklahoma City Mom blog. The blog is a platform now under a different name that exists in most major cities. Its posts are penned by local moms who volunteer their time to give opinions on various matters relating to mom life in that specific community.

Sometimes when something is meant to be, it needs to slap you across the face for you to get it. Or is that just me?

Convinced that this blog was clearly comprised of high-powered, Pulitzer Prize-winning super moms, I was sure I was never going to make it in. That night, I got my son in bed, made myself some tea (Had it not been for the fetus, it would have for sure been wine.) and wrote a post on my current life: my fears of having two kids eighteen months apart. I clicked send with an intake of breath and a prayer.

About a week later, I got an email back from the owner, saying that I'd been accepted to be a contributor and asking me to fill out the information form that she'd sent me. There was a text box for 'personal blog,' because they could take submissions from your personal blog and republish them, thereby giving you more internet credit (if you will). And I thought, *Well, no time like the present to start a personal blog.* So, *Motherhood by Meredith* was born.

It was very, very rough. I didn't know how to use WordPress to save my life. I mean, one could argue I still don't know how to use technology at all. In fact, one night I was up until 2 a.m. trying in vain to figure out how to take my home address off my newly minted website, for which it looked like a kindergartner had written the code. Yep. I was that good.

Thankfully, my writing improved faster than my ability to use technology—just ask anyone who has ever needed me to send an email with an attachment. I got better at using the critiques given to me by the editor for the moms' blog; I honed my style a little bit more.

About six months later, I was back at class, this time with a newborn in tow. I ran across that same instructor and mentioned that her simple question from that one day had changed how I was feeling. I was in the midst of battling some postpartum anxiety, dealing with extraneous emotions, but now

I had a foothold. I had something that was just for me in motherhood—something I could lean on in times of trouble. I can only explain the moment when she thought to ask that question as the Holy Spirit coming to me in the form of an athleisure-clad SAHM. (He works in mysterious ways, don't you know?)

All of the content I have ever written is inspired by my current life and the lives of those around me. Without motherhood I'd be a writer with no words.

Sometimes it's the life positions that we feel are holding us back that can actually pivot us to the new and beautiful.

Everyone has a story; it's in how you tell it.

Now some of you are sipping your coffee and saying, "Yes, girl, this is me." You have a head filled with your take on the world itching to be let out with a keyboard or bullet journal. Others of you are reading this thinking, *High school English class was the last time I wrote, and I am 100 percent okay with that.*

So, ask yourself, *What is my writing?*

What you are searching for here is an adult version of your childhood dreams that fits into your current life. Always wanted to be a rock star? Consider taking up an instrument. Wanted to be a CEO but currently feel underemployed, either with a traditional job or as the administrative assistant to a toddler? Maybe try your hand in small business.

According to a research study performed by American Express, women own 42 percent of small businesses in the United States, generating an annual profit of roughly 1.9 billion (yes, billion with a B) dollars annually (State of Women

Owned Business Report, 2019). This is a major achievement considering women weren't even involved in the work force until last century.

I do have one caveat here for moms wanting to start their own businesses. Whether you're a micro-influencer, an author, or a candle stick maker, people will try to exploit your fear of failing. I don't believe this is all deliberate, but it is the truth. If you are truly passionate about what you are doing for the greater good, then ultimately, you will not fail. Skinned knees along the way are part of the journey.

I believe that finding a passion project is vital to many women's happiness, particularly if motherhood has dramatically changed your definition of self in terms of a career. If you used to work full-time and now stay home, if you used to have a more prestigious job and took the "mommy track" (as much as I hate that terminology), you likely need something to remind you that while you love being a mom, it isn't the only part of you. I imagine this to be a similar feeling to those who retire from a lifelong career in one field and then find themselves golfing with industry insiders to keep one foot in the door. You are still a good mother if you want something in addition to motherhood. In fact, you are a better mother for recognizing that, as a human of worth, you also have needs.

I had the opportunity to chat with Jill Smokler, creator of the widely acclaimed mommy blog, *Scary Mommy*. She shared with me that creating *Scary Mommy* not only helped her stay sane as a mom of young kids but also kept her marriage intact during that time. She said, "I do think every mom needs something that's just hers." In an interview with *Your Teen Magazine,* she goes into more detail about how it felt to have three little kids and have writing as an outlet. "My mom would come over and say my house was so loud and insane and ask how I wasn't a drug addict or alcoholic, and I would say it was the blog. Whenever they were driving me crazy, I would get on and tell people and they would laugh with me, and I would feel better."

I can so relate to this with my own writing. One of the biggest things I missed from leaving my job as a nurse was the sense that I had done a good job, that I had truly helped someone that day. Of course, I help mini people I made from scratch all the time now, but it never felt quite the same. I did find that when I would write a blog post and share it, some of my favorite feedback were comments like "Me too" or "That sounds just like me." For me, blogging both replaced the feeling that I wasn't serving others to my full capacity and made me feel less alone in the struggles I faced as a new mom.

So here is my challenge to you: picture yourself as a little girl surrounded by Barbies, writing down your dreams in a Lisa Frank notebook (neon tiger on the front and all). What are you writing down? What do you want to be when you grow up? We know that things from the '80s and '90s come back around (hello scrunchies and crop tops!), so why can't your childhood dreams be the same?

One of the first thoughts that will likely enter your head is, *I don't have time for that. I'm a mom.* Friend, you have to make time. You also have to choose something as a passion project that makes you *want* to make time. If the cloud of mom guilt starts to rain on your self-growth parade, remind yourself that you are not just investing in you for you. I know we are much more motivated to do things for those around us than for ourselves.

One darling friend of mine started an embroidery business, another teaches fitness classes, and another is on the board of the YMCA. What is it that makes you feel like your soul is on fire? Did you all sing those last words like the Kings of Leon song? I sure did.

You can show your daughter that part of being a mom means you are a real human with needs and that she should find a partner who supports that. You can show your son that women are incredibly capable and deserve an equal seat at the table. You can listen to God when He tells you what His plan is for you. You may even inspire a woman around you who needs a side gig a hell of a lot more than you do. So put on your best badass, channel a little Ruth Bader Ginsburg, and get after it, girl. Bake. Run. Fail. Sew. Get up again. Sell. Write. Paint. Lead. The world needs your voice.

CHAPTER 16

SO WHAT NOW?

When you are feeling insecure about how you got pregnant and gave birth, remember babies will still go back and forth between wanting to be independent and wanting to crawl back in your uterus.

When you are feeling insecure about how you feed your baby, remember that whether they are breast- or bottle-fed, they will all grow up to prefer takeout pizza to your cooking.

When you are feeling insecure about how they sleep, imagine waking them up at 3 a.m. when they are eighteen to tell them a long and meandering story about a frog (based on a true story).

When you are feeling insecure about your parenting style, think of all the animals that literally eat their young. You are winning by not going Hannibal Lecter on their sweet selves.

When you feel the need to compare yourself to other mothers, know that some of those women want to be just like you.

When you feel social media or societal pressure to mother a certain way, listen to your kids' laughter. They couldn't care less about how closely you resemble a celebrity.

When you feel like you are falling short of perfection, know that we all are. Some days are a cake walk. Others are a marathon. You are the perfect mother for your children on the good and the hard days.

When you are struggling with your changing role and changing body as a mother, remember your favorite women from your life. Were they your favorite because of how they looked in a bikini or because of the warmth you felt from their embrace?

When you are struggling mentally as a mother, remember the best mothers are not those who do not struggle but those who seek help and show their children that Mama is human too.

When you just want someone who gets it, put yourself out there and text the mom from preschool. You can laugh about all the ridiculous things your kids say over some chips and queso.

When you feel spiritually lost, look to God, nature, or the sea to find a grounding force. You are where you are supposed to be, and you are not alone.

When you miss the woman you used to be, find something that makes the old you "you" again. And get after it.

CONCLUSION

———

While writing *Dear Jesus, Send Coffee,* I spent many nights lying in bed after tucking my babies in and worrying about the future. Worrying about what kind of mother I was that day or how I'd even get past a big hurdle in the coming weeks. I found myself praying prayers that seemed almost silly. How could a God Who created the oceans and mountains give a damn about whether Ben would always write his Ns backward or if I had scheduled enough time in between appointments the next day?

While my husband was going out daily to the front lines of COVID in the ER, I was home holding the fort without a plan and hoping we had enough toilet paper. I was glad to have something like writing to distract me from the fears of this past year, but I also had guilt. A lot of it. With my nursing background, I wondered, *Should I be working now too? I know how to take care of an ICU patient. Am I wasting that skill by being at home and working on a passion?* Of course, nursing used to be that for me. I didn't write then, though I probably should have tried it to process some of the mental load of those critically ill babies for whom I cared.

I felt heavier guilt—guilt with whipped cream on top?—in my desire to have something that was my own. Shouldn't motherhood be enough? I had chosen this life as a stay-at-home mom in congruence with my husband. I was fortunate enough to be able to make it work financially. Why was it not completely filling my cup? Did that mean there was something intrinsically wrong with me?

Through interviewing both experts, regular moms, and lots of amazing women in between, I have come to discover that the process to self-fulfillment in motherhood is both a journey and a choice.

Though we all mother in vastly different ways, many of us do experience the same kinds of insecurities in the early phases. Many of us struggled to conceive in the way we imagined or give birth on our terms. Still more of us treaded water in the oceans of advice on how to feed and parent our children on a shoestring budget of sleep.

The odds of feeling secure in our motherhood experiences are stacked against us as we attempt to shatter the ideal of perfectionism inflicted on us by social media and our own perceptions. But all hope is not lost!

While every mother I talked to had a very different life, I was surprised to learn, even in situations that appeared nothing alike, our similarities outweighed our differences. As women, we spend a lot of time looking for communities where we fit when we may actually all fit together more than we realize— our own little Motherhood Island of Misfit Toys.

We can choose to be happy or to attain the resources needed to pursue happiness—some therapy, friendships, and maybe medication—or we may not. I don't believe that one can simply will themselves from the depths of true clinical depression but choosing a positive spin over a negative one to combat the *Groundhog Day* effect of early motherhood is a choice we are all capable of making. It's not a perfect system. I have come to learn there is no such thing as perfection; even those who appear to be doing motherhood perfectly have hidden struggles.

My hope in writing this book is to help women feel less alone. Motherhood is a life-changing experience—one that simply cannot be constructed into words without living into it. I hope that you read the words of Dr. Sacks on matrescence or of Kristen Gardiner on parenting with anxiety and see a shadow of yourself. You, as God made you, are the perfect mother for your children even on days when you barely skate by. We can all strive for better, but we must also learn that guilt can hamper success more than push it. Our fears of being less than for our most important jobs as partners and mothers can make us fail to reach for our own dreams that will best utilize our precious talents.

When you feel your plate is too full and you can't handle another tantrum or middle-of-the-night feed, I encourage you to think of the community of women around the world who are living into the same experience as you. Then, Mama, bow your head and say, "Dear Jesus, send coffee."

ACKNOWLEDGEMENTS

To Ben and Avery,

Without you I would not be a mother and therefore have zero content for this book. You are raising me as a mother as I raise you.

To Travis,

Thank you for not looking at me like I had ten heads when I said I wanted to write a book in the middle of a global pandemic while you were a frontline provider. Your love and support made this possible. I love you.

To my family,

Thank you for teaching me the importance of a family rooted in love.

To the mothers that influenced me,

Thank you for teaching me that what is right is not always easy, but also that bad moments don't make bad mothers.

To my amazing interviewees,

Your stories, so graciously shared, added such richness to this experience. Thank you for your openness and vulnerability.

To Those Who Contributed to My Presale: Travis Redmon, Liz Schmittgens, Lizzie Conrad, Bre Doherty, Kate Burnley, Misty Engelbrecht, Jillian Conrad, MacKenzie Edgeman, Brandi Wiatrak, Erin Plum, Arabella Trofemuk, Elise Schrop, Megan Smith, Nicole Scholz, Cortney Kubala, Michelle Sartori, Jane Conrad, Bethanie Lied, Alene Miller, Kathy Zrike, Clare Carluccio, Yates Bryant, Marti Cook, Marci Ray, Eric Koester, Spencer Garrett, Libby Myrin, Megan Cook, Amy Gregory, Laura Colkitt, Megan Benson, Julie Johnson, Alicia Deaton, Liz Hill, Kirstin Troitino, Heather Moad, Sarah Long, Megan Kerber, Megan Peacock, Tiffany Kimbrough, Lisa Frei, Ashley Farrow, Ashley Edwards, Susie Fandos, Hannah Franklin, Illiyana Cain, Kelly Houseman, Tammie Shatzer, Katie Pettett, Michelle Muse, Jake Bevilacqua, Angie Fox-Martin, Cynthia Elkins, Syndy Redmon, Nikki Ferguson, Lauren Freeman, Diane Frei, Loralei Gann, Lauren Brownrigg, Mallory Carellas, Amy Kelley, Cathy Ellison, Andrea Cottle, Lisa Mace, and Eileen Parker.

To the NDP team,

This was both a marathon and a sprint. Thank you.

To Kaity and Dierdre,

You saw this book coming to life before I did. Thank you for helping me create it into what I hoped it would be.

APPENDIX

INTRODUCTION

Lamott, Anne. *Plan B: Further Thoughts on Faith*. New York, NY: Riverhead Books, 2006.

Murkoff, Heidi Eisenberg, Sharon Mazel, and Clifford Neppe. *What to Expect When You're Expecting*. Sydney, N.S.W.: HarperCollins Publishers, 2018.

Nonacs, R., L.S. Cohen. "Postpartum Mood Disorders: Diagnosis and Treatment Guidelines." The Journal of Clinical Psychiatry. U.S. National Library of Medicine, 1998. https://pubmed.ncbi.nlm.nih.gov/9559758/.

CHAPTER 1

"Getting Pregnant After Ovulation." American Pregnancy Association, September 23, 2020. https://americanpregnancy.org/getting-pregnant/getting-pregnant-after-ovulation-24146/.

"Infertility." Centers for Disease Control and Prevention. Centers for Disease Control and Prevention, April 13, 2021. https://www.cdc.gov/reproductivehealth/infertility/index.htm.

Johnston, Sue. *Detours: Unexpected Journeys of Hope Conceived from Infertility*. United States: Fair Winds Press, 2017.

Oster, Emily. *Expecting Better: Why the Conventional Pregnancy Wisdom Is Wrong—and What You Really Need to Know*. New York, NY: Penguin Books, 2019.

Stone, Elizabeth. *A Boy I Once Knew: What a Teacher Learned from Her Student*. New York, NY: Algonquin Books, 2013.

Tillman, Nancy. *On the Night You Were Born*. Melbourne: Vision Australia Personal Support, 2018.

CHAPTER 2

American Academy of Pediatrics. American Academy of Pediatrics, March 1, 2012. https://pediatrics.aappublications. org/content/129/3/e827.

Bonyata, Kelly. "Plugged Ducts and Mastitis." KellyMom.com, January 24, 2018. https://kellymom.com/bf/concerns/mother/ mastitis/.

Breastfeeding, Section On. "Breastfeeding and the Use of Human Milk."

Carbonneau, Elise, Véronique Provencher, Marie-Ève Labonté, Mylène Turcotte, Marie-Claude Paquette, Lyne Mongeau, Simone Lemieux, and Catherine Bégin. "A Health at Every Size Intervention Improves Intuitive Eating and Diet Quality in Canadian Women." Clinical nutrition (Edinburgh, Scotland). U.S. National Library of Medicine, June 2017. https://pubmed.ncbi.nlm.nih.gov/27378611/.

Colen, C.G., D.M. Ramey. "Is Breast Truly Best? Estimating the Effects of Breastfeeding on Long-Term Child Health and Wellbeing in the United States Using Sibling Comparisons." Journal of Social Science & Medicine (1982). U.S. National

Library of Medicine, January 29, 2014. https://pubmed.ncbi.
nlm.nih.gov/24698713/.

Mascola, Anthony J., Susan W. Bryson, and W. Stewart Agras.
"Picky Eating During Childhood: A Longitudinal Study to
Age 11 Years." *Eating Behaviors*. Pergamon, May 27, 2010.
https://www.sciencedirect.com/science/article/abs/pii/
S1471015310000528.

CHAPTER 3

"Reducing Sudden Infant Death With." AAP.org. Accessed
January 23, 2021. https://www.aap.org/en-us/advocacy-and-
policy/aap-health-initiatives/7-great-achievements/Pages/
Reducing-Sudden-Infant-Death-with-Back-to-.aspx.

"Safe Sleep Recommendations." AAP.org. Accessed January
23, 2021. https://www.aap.org/en-us/advocacy-and-policy/
aap-health-initiatives/safe-sleep/Pages/Safe-Sleep-
Recommendations.aspx.

Turgeon, Heather. *The Happy Sleeper*. Scribe Publications, 2015.

CHAPTER 4

Doyle, Glennon. *Untamed*. The Dial Press, 2020.

Li, Pamela. "What Is Attachment Parenting and What Is
Not." Parenting For Brain, April 22, 2021. https://www.
parentingforbrain.com/what-is-attachment-parenting-
attachment-theory/.

Parenting styles: An evidence-based, cross-cultural guide, 2016.
https://www.parentingscience.com/parenting-styles.html.

Power, Thomas G. "Parenting Dimensions and Styles: a Brief
History and Recommendations for Future Research."
Childhood Obesity (Print). MaryAnn Liebert, Inc.,

August 2013. https://www.ncbi.nlm.nih.gov/pmc/articles/
PMC3746212/.

Redmon, Meredith. "My Kid Has to Share and So Should Yours."
Oklahoma City Mom, April 2, 2018. https://oklahomacity.
momcollective.com/my-kid-has-to-share-and-so-should-
yours/.

CHAPTER 6

Abetz, Jenna, and Julia Moore. "'Welcome to the Mommy
Wars, Ladies': Making Sense of the Ideology of Combative
Mothering in Mommy Blogs." OUP Academic. Oxford
University Press, May 15, 2018.

https://academic.oup.com/ccc/article-
abstract/11/2/265/4996089?redirectedFrom=fulltext.

"About Cystic Fibrosis." CF Foundation. Accessed May 11, 2021.
https://www.cff.org/What-is-CF/About-Cystic-Fibrosis/.

Law, Bridget. "Biting Questions." American Psychological
Association, February 2011.

CHAPTER 7

Baker, Brenda and I. Yang. "Social Media as Social Support
in Pregnancy and the Postpartum." Sexual & reproductive
healthcare: official journal of the Swedish Association of
Midwives. U.S. National Library of Medicine, October 17,
2017. https://pubmed.ncbi.nlm.nih.gov/30193717/.

Brown, Brené. *I Thought It Was Just Me (but It Isn't): Making the
Journey from "What Will People Think?" to "I Am Enough."*
Vancouver, B.C.: Langara College, 2018.

Riccio, Christine. *Again, but Better: A Novel.* New York, NY:
Wednesday Books, 2021.

The Social Dilemma. Netflix Official Site, September 9, 2020. https://www.netflix.com/title/81254224.

Teigen, Chrissy. *Hi Again*. Medium, 14 June 2021, chrissyteigen. medium.com/hi-again-3bb3faffa76d.

Teigan, Chrissy. Twitter. Twitter. Accessed February 2, 2021. https://twitter.com/chrissyteigen?ref_ src=twsrc%5Egoogle%7Ctwcamp%5Eserp%7Ctwgr%5Eauthor.

CHAPTER 8
Dyson, Brian. "172nd Commencement Speech Georgia Tech University." September 6, 1991.

Jansen, Andrea. *The Perfect Mother Needs to Go*. Filmed: in Zurich via ZurichxTED, November 2018. https://www.ted. com/talks/andrea_jansen_the_perfect_mother_needs_to_go.

CHAPTER 9
Brown, Brené. *Gifts of Imperfection*. New York, NY: Random House Publishing Group, 2020.

"Helping Women with Postpartum Depression." PostpartumDepression.org, December 15, 2020. https://www. postpartumdepression.org/.

Hornbacher, Marya. *Wasted*. London: HarperCollins Publishers, 1999.

Kaufman, Scott Barry. *What Does It Mean to Be Self-Actualized in the 21st Century?* Scientific American Blog Network. Scientific American, November 7, 2018. https://blogs. scientificamerican.com/beautiful-minds/what-does-it-mean-to-be-self- actualized-in-the-21st-century/.

Mcleod, Saul. "Maslow's Hierarchy of Needs." Simply Psychology. Simply Psychology, December 29, 2020. https://www. simplypsychology.org/maslow.html#gsc.tab=0.

Roberts, Sam. "Dana Raphael, Proponent of Breast-Feeding and Use of Doulas, Dies at 90." *The New York Times*, February 20, 2016. https://www.nytimes.com/2016/02/21/nyregion/dana-raphael-proponent-of-breast-feeding-and-the-use-of-doulas-dies-at-90.html.

Sacks, Alexandra. "A New Way to Think about the Transition to Motherhood." Filmed New York, NY. TED, May 2018. https:// www.ted.com/talks/alexandra_sacks_a_new_way_to_think_ about_the_transi tion_to_motherhood?language=en.

Sherman-Lazar, Danielle. *Living Full: Winning My Battles with Eating Disorders.* Coral Gables, FL: Mango Publishing, 2018.

CHAPTER 10

Brown, Maressa. "Celebrity Moms Talk About Overcoming Postpartum Depression." Parents, March 4, 2020. https:// www.parents.com/baby/health/postpartum-depression/ postpartum-depression-quotes-from-celebrities/.

Osborne, Lauren M. "Postpartum Mood Disorders: What New Moms Need to Know." Johns Hopkins Medicine. Accessed March 4, 2021. https://www.hopkinsmedicine.org/health/ wellness-and-prevention/postpartum-mood- disorders-what-new-moms-need-to-know.

"Postpartum Anxiety Prevalence, Predictors and Effects on Child Development: A Review." *Journal of Psychiatry and Psychiatric Disorders. Fortune Journals*, May 2, 2017. https:// www.fortunejournals.com/articles/postpartum-anxiety-prevalence- predictors-and-effects-on-child-development-a-review.html.

CHAPTER 12

Park, Jolene. "Gray Area Drinking." Filmed TEDxCrestmoorPark via TED, November 2017.

https://www.ted.com/talks/jolene_park_gray_area_drinking?language=en.

"Positive Reframing and Examining the Evidence." Stress & Development Lab. Accessed February 16, 2021. https://sdlab.fas.harvard.edu/cognitive-reappraisal/positive-reframing-and-examining-evidence.

CHAPTER 13

"Mission / Who We Are." MOPS. Accessed February 1, 2021. https://www.mops.org/about/mission-who-we-are/.

Negron, Rennie, Anika Martin, Meital Almog, Amy Balbierz, and Elizabeth A. Howell. "Social Support during the Postpartum Period: Mothers' Views on Needs, Expectations, and Mobilization of Support." Maternal and Child Health Journal. U.S. National Library of Medicine, May 2013.https://www.ncbi.nlm.nih.gov/pmc/articles/PMC3518627/.

Rubin, Gretchen. "The Days Are Long, But the Years Are Short." Gretchen Rubin. Accessed May 17, 2021. https://gretchenrubin.com/2014/03/the-days-are-long-but-the-years-are-short/.

CHAPTER 14

Niebuhr, Reinhold, and Robert McAfee Brown. *The Essential Reinhold Niebuhr: Selected Essays and Addresses*. New Haven, CT, CT: Yale University Press, 2006.

Niequist, Shauna. *Present over Perfect: Leaving behind Frantic for a Simpler, More Soulful Way of Living*. Thorndike, ME: Center Point Large Print, 2017.

NIV Bible. Hodder & Stoughton Ltd., 2009.

The Podcast. Risen Motherhood. Accessed February 17, 2021. https://www.risenmotherhood.com/podcast.

"Religion in America: U.S. Religious Data, Demographics and Statistics." Pew Research Center's Religion & Public Life Project, September 9, 2020. https://www.pewforum.org/ religious-landscape-study/frequency-of-feeling-spiritual-peace-and-wellbeing/.

CHAPTER 15

American Express. *The State of Women-Owned Business Report,* 2019.